LINCOLN IN ILLINOIS

Commemorating the Bicentennial of the Birth of Abraham Lincoln

February 12, 2009

Ron Schramm
Photographer

Richard E. Hart
Compiler and Editor

The Abraham Lincoln Association

First paperback edition January 2009.

ISBN: 978-0-9818329-2-0

Cover Photograph: *Head of State,* Augustus Saint-Gaudens, May 31, 1926, Grant Park, Court of Presidents, north of Congress Parkway near Columbus Drive, Chicago, Illinois

Design and Layout: Creativille, Inc., Edwardsville, Illinois

THE ABRAHAM LINCOLN ASSOCIATION

The purpose of The Abraham Lincoln Association is to observe each anniversary of the birth of Abraham Lincoln, to preserve and make more accessible the landmarks associated with his life, and actively to encourage, promote, and aid the collection and dissemination of authentic information regarding all phases of his life and career.

ACKNOWLEDGEMENTS

The Abraham Lincoln Association gratefully acknowledges
the generous support and assistance of the organizations listed below.
Publication of this book is made possible in part by their support.

THE ABRAHAM LINCOLN PRESIDENTIAL LIBRARY FOUNDATION

THE ILLINOIS ABRAHAM LINCOLN BICENTENNIAL COMMISSION

THE ILLINOIS DEPARTMENT OF COMMERCE AND ECONOMIC DEVELOPMENT, TOURISM DIVISION

ILLINOIS. MILE AFTER MAGNIFICENT MILE.

Table of Contents

THE PHOTOGRAPHS

Table of Contents

THE SCULPTORS

Table of Contents

THE COMMENTATORS

PREFACE

We all know him. We use his name for our schools, parks, libraries, streets and businesses. We form organizations to perpetuate his memory and build museums to display his story. We preserve the places where he worked and lived and collect his personal items. Some write books about him while others collect those books. A few of you create sculptures of his person. He was Abraham Lincoln, and we commemorate his 200th birthday with this book of photographs of his Illinois statues.

In 1952, The Abraham Lincoln Association published *Lincoln in Marble and Bronze* by F. Lauriston Bullard. At that time, Bullard stated that there were fifteen "Lincolns" in Illinois. His book describing those fifteen statues was 356 pages long. When photographer Ron Schramm wrote to the Association suggesting a photographic record of all of the Lincoln statues in Illinois, I thought that perhaps the number would have doubled to thirty statues. In fact there are at least eighty, and there are more in various stages of planning and creation.

The oldest of the statues is *The Emancipator* by Larkin G. Mead. The statue stands at the base of the oblisk at the Lincoln Tomb in Springfield's Oak Ridge Cemetery and was dedicated on October 15, 1874. There are older Lincoln busts, the oldest being *Lincoln the President* by Thomas Dow Jones, created in January 1861.

As I write this, I hesitate to designate the most recent statue as there are at least five scheduled for completion and dedication during the Bicentennial year—2009. Thinking it best to leave no town or statue behind, I have included photographs of statues and busts not yet dedicated but either cast or in the maquette stage of the sculptor's creative process. For example, the bust *Prairie Lawyer—Master of Us All* has been cast and will stand in the Great Hall of the Illinois Supreme Court. Metamora's *Out of Court* has been cast and will stand before the Metamora Courthouse. Bloomington's *Lincoln, Fell, and Davis in Bloomington* and Hillsboro's *Among Friends* have not yet been cast, but photographs of the sculptors' maquettes have been included. All of these are scheduled for dedication in 2009.

The style of the statues and busts runs from the monumental and heroic Lincoln to the homespun and almost comedic Lincoln.

The photographs are accompanied by comments from a variety of people giving their impressions when looking at one of the photographs. Their impressions are not intended to be artistic criticism or historical analysis, but rather personal responses. How does the statue make you feel? What does it prompt you to remember? A Lincoln Rorschach test. The comments, like the statues, run the gamut from heroic to humorous prose. Such is the nature of our man. We all look at his images and are moved in many different ways.

It has been a pleasure to work with Ron Schramm and all of the commentators. I am most appreciative of the assistance and encouragement given to this project by Tom Schwartz, Illinois State Historian. Editorial review by Erin Bishop and James Cornelius has been most helpful. Carl Volkmann and David Wiegers generously shared their extensive knowledge of Illinois' Lincoln statues. Publication of this book was made possible in part by the Abraham Lincoln Presidential Library Foundation, the Illinois Abraham Lincoln Bicentennial Commission and the Illinois Department of Commerce and Economic Development, Tourism Division. Thanks to all of you.

We hope that all will enjoy this 200th birthday tribute to the greatest American—Abraham Lincoln.

Richard E. Hart
President
The Abraham Lincoln Association

Illinois is Lincoln-land. Nearly every city and town in the state has a Lincoln street, or a Lincoln square, or a Lincoln park, or a Lincoln school. Hundreds—perhaps thousands—of businesses are plastered with his name. In the city directory of Chicago the list runs from the Lincoln Antique Mall to Lincoln Heating and Air Conditioning to Lincoln Mechanics and so on through the rest of the alphabet. The bustling county seat of Logan County is named Lincoln; as a young man Abraham Lincoln surveyed the site and laid out the streets. Appropriately, it is the home of the flourishing Lincoln College. The meticulously restored village where Lincoln spent his formative years is called Lincoln's New Salem. Springfield boasts, among many Lincoln sites, the Lincoln Home, the Lincoln-Herndon Law Office, and the Lincoln Tomb. Most impressive of all is the huge Abraham Lincoln Presidential Library and Museum.

Throughout the state dozens of statues—mostly at county seats or in towns where Lincoln delivered one of his immortal speeches—pay tribute to the Sixteenth President. Lincoln in Illinois presents photographs of most of these statues, each coupled with a brief commentary from a variety of people. These are not intended to be detailed histories or esthetic evaluations but are offered as personal meditations evoked by the statues.

Though these sculptures differ considerably in concept and execution, all of the sculptors faced similar problems. All found it difficult to carve a free-standing male figure that does not topple over. Realizing this problem, previous artists had generally presented men who were, in effect, propped up by the long, flowing robes they wore, or by the arms they carried, or by convenient tree trunks. But, except in Avard Fairbanks's statue of a very young man with musket, Lincoln did not lend himself to such treatment. Many of the sculptors of necessity placed him on what is obviously a very sturdy bench or chair.

Apart from that, the sculptors had difficulty with Lincoln's unusual figure. Six feet and four inches in height, he was lanky as well as tall; his chest was narrow, his legs disproportionately long, and his feet very large. There was also the question of how to treat his face. Illinois residents remembered smooth-shaven Lincoln, for he had no beard until late 1860, but Americans generally thought of him as the bewhiskered figure on their currency.

Sculptors were also frustrated by the fact that Lincoln's face changed so much with his moods. When he was unhappy or when he was obliged to pose for a picture, he looked sad, almost forlorn. One Massachusetts soldier who encountered him in this mood called him "the ugliest man I ever put my eyes on." But when he was in good spirits, an Ohio congressman reported, his face brightened "like a lit lantern ... [and] his dull eyes would fairly sparkle with fun."

With such a difficult subject some sculptors simply gave up and abandoned their incomplete statues. But what is most striking about the sculptures that were completed is the respect, bordering on reverence, with which Lincoln is presented. Good, bad, or indifferent as works of art, all show a man who is kindly, good humored, far-seeing, and wise. Those are traits that Americans have enshrined in their hearts, and they help explain why Illinois has so many statues of Lincoln today.

David Herbert Donald

When I began this work, I despaired of making a worthy or satisfactory statue. So many, almost all, of the likenesses of Lincoln represent him as ungainly, uncouth, homely, unpicturesque; but when I had made a study of his life, had learned more and more of his character, of his natural nobility and lovableness, his deep and true human sympathy, had read of him, talked of him with men who knew him and loved him, I became more and more convinced that his face must have been the most truly beautiful of all I have tried to model.

Augustus Saint-Gaudens

LINCOLN IN ILLINOIS

Portion of speech delivered in Springfield on February 10, 2007

This campaign has to be about reclaiming the meaning of citizenship, restoring our sense of common purpose, and realizing that few obstacles can withstand the power of millions of voices calling for change.

By ourselves, this change will not happen. Divided, we are bound to fail.

But the life of a tall, gangly, self-made Springfield lawyer tells us that a different future is possible.

He tells us that there is power in words.

He tells us that there is power in conviction.

That beneath all the differences of race and region, faith and station, we are one people.

He tells us that there is power in hope.

As Lincoln organized the forces arrayed against slavery, he was heard to say this: "Of strange, discordant, and even hostile elements, we gathered from the four winds, and formed and fought to battle through."

That is our purpose here today.

That is why I'm in this race.

Not just to hold an office, but to gather with you to transform a nation.

I want to win that next battle — for justice and opportunity.

I want to win that next battle — for better schools, and better jobs, and better health care for all.

I want us to take up the unfinished business of perfecting our union, and building a better America.

And if you will join with me in this improbable quest, if you feel destiny calling, and see as I see, a future of endless possibility stretching before us; if you sense, as I sense, that the time is now to shake off our slumber, and slough off our fear, and make good on the debt we owe past and future generations, then I am ready to take up the cause, and march with you, and work with you. Today, together, we can finish the work that needs to be done, and usher in a new birth of freedom on this Earth.

Barack Obama

Lincoln the Man
Augustus Saint-Gaudens
October 22, 1887

Lincoln Park
Clark Street and North Avenue
Chicago, Illinois

In this majestic statue depicting Abraham Lincoln as *Head of State*, Saint-Gaudens creates a powerful image of dignity, isolation, strength, and sorrow. Lincoln's gaunt head is tilted down, as if the pressures of the office had driven his thoughts downward and inward. The long fingers of his right hand are spread upon his right knee. The left hand clenches into a fist on the ornate arm of his flag-draped throne. He gazes down in a grim and almost forbidding manner. The emotion created is one of stillness and solitary power. The great majority of the images we see of Lincoln suggest a similar feeling of sorrow, solitude, and depth.

Yet, the Lincoln I sensed after living with him for more than a decade—from his own words and the myriad letters, diaries, and descriptions of others—was a surprisingly vibrant man with a life-affirming sense of humor and an unparalleled gift for storytelling. The statue I would most love to see would depict the mirthful eyes and expressive hands of Lincoln the storyteller, standing with his back against a fire in a tavern, entertaining a crowd of mesmerized listeners for hours with one winding tale after another, rather than the grim solitude of the enthroned sage. It was said that his "eyes would sparkle with fun and when he reached the point in his narrative which invariably evoked the laughter of the crowd," he would lean forward and slap his hand on his knee, for "nobody's enjoyment was greater than his." He laughed, he explained, so he did not weep. His stories were intended "to whistle off sadness." How I would love to see him laughing, for then he would truly come alive!

Doris Kearns Goodwin

Head of State
Augustus Saint-Gaudens
May 31, 1926

Grant Park
Court of Presidents, north of Congress Parkway near Columbus Drive
Chicago, Illinois

This statue doesn't show Old Abe, the brooding, melancholy statesman, but A. Lincoln, the gangly-legged lawyer who won courtroom, boardroom, and public platform battles, and now brims with confidence, polish, and even chic.

Observe his stance: this is no longer a man who is shy or uncertain. He is no longer a home-schooled prairie lawyer, who learned his trade reading deep into the night by flickering candlelight in a general store. He is a sharp, shrewd, and practiced litigator who has become rich. He is one of the nation's foremost advocates, and has become a clarion voice against slavery. He has been tested by life, and learned from his experience. He knows he is the equal of any man he has met (including Stephen A. Douglas), and any that he is likely to encounter (think: George McClellan). I would say that if you look at his face, you almost hear Lincoln say, "Bring it on," except that this phrase is in bad repute right now.

And mark the gaze. Lincoln was tall. It is not likely that his elevated gaze was fixed on another person. It locked on a point over the horizon, in the future. Locked on, dare I suggest, the history that he will make.

Scott Simon

The Great Chicago Lincoln
Avard Fairbanks
October 20, 1956

Confluence of Lincoln, Lawrence, and Western avenues
Chicago, Illinois

Abraham Lincoln believed in what historian Gabor Boritt has called the "right to rise." Charles Keck's sculpture *The Young Lincoln* embodies both Lincoln's aspiration to rise and also his homespun humility. The Chicago statue portrays Lincoln looking outward, toward the horizon, implying the foresight which would characterize his speeches and his statesmanship.

Young Lincoln had little access to the formal curriculum of college-educated elites. What Lincoln read on his own, he mastered—the Bible, Shakespeare, Blackstone's Commentaries, Euclid's geometry. "If I like a thing, it just sticks, after once reading it or hearing it," Lincoln said. Nothing stuck so fast to the sixteenth president as the Declaration of Independence. This fundamental document, the Act of Union, he probably read first in the statute books of early Indiana, where he grew up. In Charles Keck's bronze, we see clearly the manuscript he grasps, suggesting Lincoln's grip on the principles of the Declaration of Independence, which anchored his public life.

With his extraordinary Peoria Speech of October 16, 1854, Lincoln inaugurated his anti-slavery campaign designed to restore the "equality principle" of the American founding enshrined in the Declaration of Independence. A similar speech in Chicago in late October of the same year led one local newspaper to report what Keck's statue implies—how Lincoln overcame "the trials of poverty and by the sweat of his brow…[how he became] the most powerful speaker and one of the ablest lawyers in the West."

Lewis E. Lehrman

The Young Lincoln
Charles Keck
Placed in 1997

Senn Park
Clark Street and Ridge Boulevard
Chicago, Illinois

Lincoln's image as prodigious rail splitter may be as carefully hewn as the statue bearing that name.

As a young man, Lincoln undoubtedly helped his family build a cabin and the requisite split-rail fence. His prowess at rail-splitting, however, may be more myth than reality.

Three decades after Lincoln split his last rail, the then-presidential candidate was told by a friend that his well-known but colorless "Honest Abe" sobriquet needed an enhancement.

The new image of homesteading frontiersman was unveiled in time for the 1860 Republican National Convention, when Lincoln (by then a powerful corporate lawyer) was portrayed as the strong, dynamic, unpretentious rail splitter from the West.

The image became enormously popular with delegates, who launched Lincoln on his destiny to preserve the union.

Years later, in the midst of national crisis, Lincoln showed that he never lost his acumen for totin' chip.

In the waning days of the Civil War, the Great Emancipator visited a battlefield, where an ax lay across a log. The President smiled, grabbed the heavy ax with his right hand, and held it horizontally for a few minutes, without a quiver.

After he left, several muscular soldiers tried to repeat the President's feat. None could.

Jesse Jackson, Jr.

Lincoln the Rail Splitter
Charles James Mulligan
September 12, 1911

Garfield Park
Washington Boulevard and Central Park
Chicago, Illinois

Here, in a battered and neglected African-American neighborhood, in the promised land of Chicago's South Side, stares out at us a battered, neglected, and forlorn face of Abraham Lincoln, an unintended metaphor, perhaps, for the place of Lincoln in early twenty-first century African-American thinking. Once, as a monument to the Freedmen's Bureau, the image of the Great Emancipator was cast out of pennies, the widow's mite of black children whose parents had been freed . . .

Freed by Lincoln?

There's the question. The promise of freedom was certainly betrayed after his death. So much so that Lincoln's own commitment to Black Freedom became almost laughable to many. (As if white men cared.) A new art and style arose. African roots were celebrated. Who will polish the marble of the "white man's president" now?

But for how long? Responding to the challenge of Black Power scholarship, recent scholars have been dusting off Lincoln and buffing out a more genuine, if also more complex, anti-slavery shine. And perhaps the advent of our first African-American president may also help restore some of Lincoln's former luster.

Lincoln waits in that abandoned lot; waits for all of us.

Stewart Winger

Lincoln
Phillip Bloomquist
1926

69th Street and Wolcott Avenue (formerly Lincoln Street)
Chicago, Illinois

Among the many talents for which Abraham Lincoln is revered, the most enduring may be his eloquence. A lawyer by trade, Lincoln grasped intricacy. He also had a bard's sense of meter and economy. His 1863 Gettysburg Address remains the most stunning presidential oration in our country's history, a shotglass measure of emotion and leadership at a time of upheaval. Lincoln accomplished this in under 300 words (around the length of this entry), displaying a typical laconic elegance in commemorating the Civil War dead at the Soldiers' National Cemetery.

It is fitting, then, that we find Charles James Mulligan's statue of *Lincoln the Orator* in another graveyard, Chicago's Oak Woods Cemetery, the burial place for 6,000 Confederate prisoners of war who died at nearby Camp Douglas. Oak Woods is also the final resting place for civil rights pioneers Jesse Owens, Ida Wells, and Harold Washington, the first African American mayor of Chicago. Here, Lincoln stands between two rows of simple tombstones, reaching his right hand aloft as if to impart a rhetorical point or, perhaps, commission souls heavenward. The reserved president may never have gestured in such dramatic fashion. But the resilience of his words has little to do with his performance as a speaker — he was considered pinched and high-pitched, with an inscrutably Midwestern accent. What gives his language such lasting power is its passion and precision. Speaking at Gettysburg, he said:

"[W]e cannot dedicate - we cannot consecrate - we cannot hallow - this ground. The brave men, living and dead, who struggled here, have consecrated it far above our poor power to add or subtract. The world will little note nor long remember what we say here, but it can never forget what they did here."

That is true only in part, for Lincoln's words are unforgettable.

Luke O'Brien

Lincoln the Orator
Charles James Mulligan
1905

Oak Woods Cemetery
Chicago, Illinois

Historical sculptor Gary Casteel was commissioned to produce an outdoor piece for the Kentucky state memorial at the Civil War battlefield at Vicksburg, Mississippi. He chose the two sons of Kentucky, each of whom became the leader of his respective portion of the country during that "brothers" war.

The original vision for the dual sculpture was the reconciliation of North and South through the full-size, standing images of Abraham Lincoln and Jefferson Davis.

Yet, for me, Casteel has instead captured a steadfast and determined Lincoln as Commander-in-Chief. Careworn certainly; and with hat in hand—gentle reminder of his humility and undertone of caring. But he was resolute on the basic issues of the day. As far as Union was concerned, there would be no reconciliation until after unconditional surrender and a re-establishment of that Union, and without slavery, after Emancipation. He certainly did not countenance Davis's being considered an equal president of any portion of the "united" states.

This particular bronze statue was the only duplicate taken from the original mold before that was destroyed. The patina is warm and rich, drawing the viewer toward contemplation—and a thankfulness that he was there to save that union.

The statue stands in the front window of the Abraham Lincoln Book Shop, Inc. in Chicago, beckoning the curious to enter the fascinating world of Lincolniana.

Daniel R. Weinberg

President Lincoln
Gary Casteel
Circa 2004

Abraham Lincoln Bookshop
357 West Chicago Avenue
Chicago, Illinois

The sturdy dignity that characterizes Carl Tolpo's *Presidential Lincoln* (completed in 1957) was partially a response to the sculptor's thoroughly middle-class, mid-twentieth-century anxiety that subversive elements in modern culture sought to "divorce art from morality so that the artist has no wholesome influence on society." Tolpo, for instance, protested against placing a Picasso sculpture in downtown Chicago, believing that Picasso's modern style was "grotesque." This forty-two-inch-high heroic Lincoln bust was Tolpo's attempt to "make [art] mean something in a positive sense." Its larger-than-life stolid countenance evoked the high moral grandeur of Gutzon Borglum's Mt. Rushmore Lincoln (Borglum had taken a special interest in Tolpo's early career—even giving him chisels used on Mt. Rushmore). From this photographic perspective Tolpo's Lincoln appears to be a blockish, one-dimensional Lincoln caricature. But from other vantage points the sculpture's shadowing and subtle facial linings reveal a more complex and nuanced visage—metaphorically suggesting the complex, multidimensional nature of the human flesh-and-blood Lincoln of history, as well as the complex and multifaceted nature of the sculptor's mid-twentieth-century American world that has sometimes been simplistically caricatured as a time of rigid one-dimensional conformity.

Bryon C. Andreasen

Presidential Lincoln
Carl Tolpo
1957

Barrington High School
Barrington, Illinois

Doris Kearns Goodwin can see the statuary twinkle in Lincoln's eyes as they look out over the backyard of sculptor Fran Volz. In the tradition of Daniel Chester French's Lincoln, and very deeply so, Volz's Lincoln is, however, not in the medium for which Volz is best known: snow. Nor is it in French's marble. Volz chose the less seasonal and less weighty polyfoam. Thus, at half the height of French's Lincoln and much lighter, it travels—unlike most Lincoln statues—mostly to malls, though not the sort upon which French's Lincoln looks so solemnly. But this is good. Lincoln in the atrium would inspire ideals of a higher sort than shopping, if only for a moment. That moment, times the frequency of the occurrence, might transform the experience of the millions in the malls of America every day.

Laurin A. Wollan, Jr.

Replica of the Lincoln Memorial
Fran Volz
August 2007

Residence of Fran Volz
Arlington Heights Road
Arlington Heights, Illinois

Heads Up: Abe Returns to Niles Resting Spot

Public Works crews were up early Tuesday morning re-installing a Niles landmark in his rightful place. The life-size statue of Abraham Lincoln that normally sits outside on a couch across the street from the Niles Police Department was returned to his spot after a month "vacation" while his head was reattached to his body.

"Abe Lincoln's back! All is right with the world," joked Village Manager George Van Geem.

The statue was decapitated Sept. 22 when Michael Orlando of Wood Dale, 27, was posing for pictures following a wedding ceremony that afternoon. "The wedding party was leaning against it," said Niles Police Staff Sgt. Tom Davis. "Someone got a little rough with it, and knocked the head off."

An observant bystander immediately called Niles police to report the potential theft of Abe Lincoln's cabeza as it disappeared into a wedding limo and headed north on Milwaukee Avenue.

The limo was stopped by police shortly after. Members of the wedding party claimed they were on the way to the station across the street to return the displaced head.

Orlando was issued a ticket for damage to village property. The head may have fallen off easily after sustaining previous damage, said police.

Orlando must appear in Niles court Nov. 15 to answer for his actions concerning the dead president's noggin.

In the meantime Niles residents can breathe a sigh of relief that they won't have to worry about a headless Lincoln haunting Milwaukee Avenue this Halloween.

The statue was donated to Niles from the City of Chicago "couches" exhibit several years ago, said village officials. If the entire statue, couch and all, vanishes in coming weeks, don't panic. It's just been taken down for the winter.

Daniel Cameron
The Journal & Topics Newspapers
Des Plaines, Illinois
Wednesday, October 24, 2007

Just Don't Sit There, Do Something
Jeff P. Garland
2001

Milwaukee and Touhy Avenues
Niles, Illinois

Reminiscent of the February 1864 photograph taken at Mathew Brady's studio in Washington, D. C., Rebecca Caleel's sculpture of Lincoln and son Tad that is displayed at the Oak Brook Public Library captures the spirit of the "connection" that is made when parents read to their children. There is an inexplicable joy that results when families read together … parent to child … child to parent.

Libraries across the State of Illinois participate in an annual "Family Reading Night" but libraries support the encouragement, joy, and love of reading throughout the year. There are reading programs for every interest and every age. From preschoolers to seniors, libraries offer books and materials that can transport readers to places they can often only dream about.

Despite what was happening on that day in 1864, President Lincoln made the time, took the time to read to Tad, to spend time with Tad. I wonder what book they're reading? I wonder if Tad is enjoying it? I can only imagine that they are enjoying their time together and enjoying each other's company…

The time spent reading together is time to be cherished.

Kathryn M. Harris

Lincoln and Son
Rebecca Childers Caleel
June 2004

Oak Brook Public Library
Oak Brook, Illinois

On an early March day in 1832, Abraham Lincoln tossed his hat into the political arena for the first time. Self-taught, Lincoln understood the power of education, and for much of his life remained a life-long learner. Announcing his plans to run for office, Lincoln declared in a circular that March day, "I view it [education] as the most important subject which we as a people can be engaged in." Thus it is appropriate that Avard Fairbanks's sculpture *Lincoln the Friendly Neighbor* stands on the grounds of the Lincoln School in Berwyn. As a teacher the image tugs at me. A kindly and warm Abraham Lincoln, arms draped around a little boy and little girl, shepherds them into their future, guiding them it seems to something he lacked—a formal education. But truth be told, in this age of educational labels, were Lincoln a student in my classroom he would bear the sobriquet "gifted child."

I too am drawn to the quote etched into the pedestal, "The better part of one's life consists of his friendships." Lincoln was a good man and as much as he understood the power of education he also valued relationships, seeking, even with his enemies, to cultivate the best possible circumstances between individuals. Schools are a place where lifetime friendships are formed, bonds that help shape who we become. Here, before Fairbanks's handiwork, Lincoln imparts important life lessons for all of us.

James A. Percoco

Lincoln the Friendly Neighbor
Avard Fairbanks
July 4, 1959

Lincoln School
Berwyn, Illinois

In my research it appeared that Lincoln was always portrayed as a sad, lonely, and serious man. I decided that my representation of him would not bear this image. During the Civil War, this nation was under a great deal of stress and turmoil. I felt in my heart that there had to be some happy moments in Lincoln's life so I decided to concentrate on those moments when Lincoln might have been at peace and happy.

What better way to express a moment of happiness than having children present. The decision to place this sculpture at the Crossroads of the Nation—Lincoln Highway and Dixie Highway in Chicago Heights, Illinois—gave me the inspiration to use the Mayor's, at that time, Mr. Sam Ciambrone, niece. When planning this I learned that she had a sister and I decided to use her also so she would not be unhappy at being excluded.

My concept of using the girls to present Mr. Lincoln a bouquet of flowers was to express the hopes in their eyes that he would have the courage to lead this nation out of darkness and turmoil. Also, his carrying the Bible symbolizes the strength, guidance, and humanity he gained from relying on his faith.

There have been few presidents that have exemplified the strength of character needed to lead this nation. Abraham Lincoln was certainly one of the greatest, and that is what I learned and tried to convey in my sculpture.

Giovanni Bucci

On the Road to Greatness
Giovanni Bucci
2003

Intersection of the Lincoln Highway and the Dixie Highway
Chicago Heights, Illinois

People associate Abe with Illinois and its history, making his image a perfect icon along one of Illinois's major highways, I-57.

Travelers often stop to have their pictures taken with *Abe*. He has become a local landmark, quite appropriate for the state with the motto "Land of Lincoln." Lincoln had many hard decisions to make while in office—time has proven him to be correct even though there was a terrible price to pay.

I personally admire Lincoln and his principles and erected this statue as a tribute. Travelers can admire a twenty-nine-foot high statue on a ten-foot base. *Abe* always has a message in his left hand that changes every three to four weeks that he would approve of—"No New Taxes." "Support Our Troops." "Merry Christmas." "Abe was a Republican." "God Bless America."

Jerry Alexander

Abe
Jerry Vettrus
2004

Alexander Equipment Rental, Inc.
1511 Commerce Drive
Exit 315, Interstate 57
Bourbonnais, Illinois

Set atop a fifteen-foot high pedestal, Carl Tolpo's Lincoln bust is formal and stately. The statue is located in an inner court of the Lake County Court House, although now, in this post-9/11 world, sadly cordoned off and inaccessible to the public.

Looking straight ahead at the statue, I see that Lincoln is serious and pensive; looking from either side, however, he seems amused, with a slight smile on his face. From all angles, however, the large shock of hair on his forehead dominates the view.

On both sides of the massive pedestal are friezes relating stories tying in Waukegan to Lincoln and the Civil War. Within ten days of the opening of hostilities at Fort Sumter, a group of eighty-four volunteers had left Waukegan to join fighting regiments who were forming in Chicago.

Willard Bunn

Presidential Lincoln
Carl Tolpo, Bust
1977
Lily Tolpo, Panels
1995

Plaza
Lake County Couthouse
Waukegan, Illinois

This is Lincoln the Illinois lawyer, "Honest Abe," ready and eager to debate Stephen A. Douglas in 1858 in my hometown where the "Freeport Question" somehow grew into legendary importance. Freeport was the site of their most important debate. Lincoln was the leading man of the Illinois Republican Party. He was serious, purposeful, strong, and very much a man of the people. Here is the pre-presidential Lincoln without the cares and worries of the Civil War. Looking back on him from the 21st century, I don't see how the country could have survived without him. He deserves a statue that is larger than life-size.

The statue was a gift to the people from W. T. Rawleigh, who, like Lincoln, was a self-made man.

Robert J. Lenz

Lincoln the Debater
Leonard Crunelle
August 27, 1929

Taylor Park
Freeport, Illinois

Abraham Lincoln posed his momentous "Freeport Question" to Stephen Douglas during their second joint debate on August 27, 1858: "Can the people of a United States Territory, in any lawful way, against the wish of any citizen of the United States, exclude slavery from its limits prior to the formation of a State Constitution?" In their first debate at Ottawa a week earlier, Douglas had asked Lincoln a series of questions designed to put him on the defensive. "The fire flew some," Lincoln admitted, "and I am glad to know I am yet alive." At Freeport, Lincoln decided to strike back with a question of his own that he knew the Little Giant could not possibly answer without risking his bid for the Senate or sacrificing his claim to the presidency two years later. On this chilly, gray afternoon, ten to fifteen thousand people poured into Freeport and strained forward intently to hear the two men debate the future of freedom and democracy. The crowd applauded Lincoln as he asked his question, destined to become the most famous single sentence uttered in all of his joint debates with Douglas. Sitting serenely on the three-foot-high square platform on this spot that now seemed "jammed with humanity," Lincoln listened patiently as Douglas delivered his impassioned reply.

Kenneth J. Winkle

Lincoln and Douglas in Debate
Lily Tolpo
August 27, 1992

Debate Square
Near North State Avenue and East Douglas Street
Freeport, Illinois

From high above, the freakishly long sinewy arm of Abraham Lincoln thrusts out into the air. The muscles and tendons in his right arm bulge and ache with the effort. His right hand is placed, palm upwards.

What is he reaching for? Is he giving us something or waiting for something to be placed in his hand?

Chief Black Hawk or Ma-ca-tai-me-she-kia-kiak of the Sauk tribe clings precariously to this Mother Rock, his body precariously perched atop a large golden bronze rock. He stretches every muscle in his body upwards as he thrusts his right arm and his robe upward. His toes and the fingers of his left hand nearly dig into the metal so that he won't slide off.

What is he reaching for? What is he grasping at?

There is something about this statue that grabs the viewer and pulls him closer. Even before you are near enough to it to discern the details of the piece it is evident that something or someone is reaching out to you and pulling you near. As you step up to the piece, you are taken by the amount of detail in the statue. Each figure is powerful in his own right but, together, they form a work more powerful than either alone.

In this Jeff Adams piece, featuring a young Abraham Lincoln and Chief Black Hawk, the famous pair is not the typical static and stiff subjects that we have come to expect in works of art featuring historical characters.

This is one of the most dramatic depictions of Abraham Lincoln that you will ever see. The juxtaposition of Lincoln and Black Hawk is unique and right.

David B. Wiegers

Paths of Conviction, Footsteps of Fate
Jeff Adams
October 13, 2002

Mix Park
Route 2
Oregon, Illinois

As Carl Sandburg said about Abraham Lincoln and his fellow countrymen on the 150th birthday of Abraham Lincoln, "...this country has always had them in crises—men and women who understand that wherever there is freedom, there have been those who fought, toiled, and sacrificed for it." This aptly describes Lincoln. As this sculpture depicts, he was a patriot in the deepest sense of the word, and embodied loyalty in a way that is sorely lacking in today's society. As a volunteer soldier in the Black Hawk War in Illinois, his experience provided him with the strength and character that he needed in the years ahead.

Lincoln was elected by his fellow volunteers as captain, and although he was inexperienced as a military leader, Lincoln did his best to instill discipline in his company. In his later years, when Lincoln alluded to his time of service, he told his listeners that he saw no combat, but "had a good many bloody struggles with the mosquitoes."

Most importantly, Lincoln never forgot his military service during his time as commander-in-chief; he had an appreciation of the soldier's life and remembered what it was like to wait for rations and pay and sleep on the cold ground. Indeed, he reflected that no subsequent success in his life gave him as much satisfaction as when he volunteered in the militia and was elected captain of his company. Little did he know at the time that he would become a great captain, presiding over a country torn asunder.

Frank J. Williams

Captain Lincoln in the Black Hawk War
Leonard Crunelle
August 23, 1930

Fort Dixon
Just off Galena Street (Route 26)
Dixon, Illinois

In July 1856 Abraham Lincoln criss-crossed northern Illinois stumping for the Republican cause. Less than a month before, delegates at the first Republican convention had considered him for vice president on the party's first presidential ticket. On July 18 he appeared at "a grand rally" in Sterling. He came at the behest of an old political associate, Robert L. Wilson of the famed "Long Nine," the group that had spearheaded moving the state capital to Springfield in 1837.

The previous day Lincoln had spoken at nearby Dixon. A correspondent described him as "crooked-legged, stoop-shouldered, spare-built, and anything but handsome in the face." But appearances could be deceptive: "as a close observer and cogent reasoner, he has few equals and perhaps no superior in the world. His language is pure and respectful, he attacks no man's character or motives, but fights with arguments."

We don't know what Lincoln said at Sterling, but we can imagine him, newspaper in hand, earnestly making his case. It may have been "a grand rally" in the summer of 1856, but now he stands solitary before the occasional visitor. We find ourselves looking up, as if we are ready to listen to what he has to say ... for Lincoln still speaks to us.

Brooks D. Simpson

Lincoln in Sterling
Don Morris
July 18, 2006

Propheter Park
Sterling, Illinois

This bronze bust was cast by the Florentine Brotherhood Foundry, to stand near the gate of the Union Stockyards in Chicago. Now it poses at the center of town before a lovely old brick manse, today the town Historical Museum. It is a town of a size which allows birds and rabbits to swarm around Mr. Lincoln, while at some hours the street before him is parked solid. And whereas the Fjelde bust once inspired heavy work, from 1916 to 1971, it has inspired thoughtful repose here since a benefactor moved it in 1997. A garden, a lawn, a collection of local history and life is its bailiwick now. Is this the new trajectory of Lincoln in American memory? The garden in back is filling with plaques to the many devoted volunteers in local history.

But no. In Europe such a house (at least between May and September) would be a monument to its owner, and to a heraldic lineage. In the Midwest, the home and the statue before it represent, like the American nation, a striving after an ideal. Yet neither home nor museum is a mere ideal, time-out-of-mind. The original of this Fjelde replica stands in Frogner Park, in Oslo, Norway, where silent marchers gathered by it each fourth of July during their years of Nazi occupation, 1940-45. Sometimes a statue inspires local memory; sometimes it guards.

James M. Cornelius

Lincoln Bust at Geneseo
Paul Fjelde
1916
June 15, 1997

Geneseo Historical Musuem
205 S. State Street
Geneseo, Illinois

The hands are what reach out first.

From almost as soon as he could lift things, Lincoln's hands were hefting axes, mauls, rails, scythes, wrestlers, and by adulthood, they had become huge, rough, and powerful.

The weights those hands heave here are ideas—law, freedom, equality. They seem at first to beckon, as in some kind of invitation. But a glance at Lincoln's face, set and determined to the border of grimness, and at Douglas's glowering fury, clenched fists, and boxer's stand, show that Lincoln's gesture is instead a summons. The hands demand that all the forces of error and slavery which Douglas has disguised as truth, come for a close grappling which will expose their corrosive nature. They will pit every ounce of the strength they have against the silent brutishness of despotism.

Come, the hands say, I will show you where we are and whither we are tending.

Allen C. Guelzo

Lincoln-Douglas Debate
Rebecca Childers Caleel
September 14, 2002

Washington Square Park
Ottawa, Illinois

There was a time when they had all been together.

Under a clear sky, in the lee of a young maple tree, Mary and Abraham Lincoln are standing together watching their children play—all of the family appearing as silhouettes upon a twilight landscape. Soon the fireflies will come bearing their cryptic messages.

Mary has taken her husband's hand as if to lead him away, while she reaches out for the boys, Willie and Tad, to join them. The bright day is almost over. Time to quit their game of swordplay, put down the maple wands; time to leave Springfield, Illinois, the green prairie, the Sangamon River, the dog, the milk cow, the house they call home.

Time to follow the president-elect to Washington and their destiny, the nation's capital, the White House; to ride through cheering crowds to glory and agony, the anguish of Civil War, the house of death and eternity where their own human shadows and the inhuman night everlasting will become one.

There was a time when they had been happy, a twilight as fleeting as the passage of fireflies.

Daniel Mark Epstein

Traveling the I & M Canal
Marsha Lega
2006

Lock 14 of the Illinois and Michigan Canal
LaSalle, Illinois

What the sculptor Avard Fairbanks almost certainly wanted to convey in the bas-relief designed for Knox College's Old Main is Abraham Lincoln's steely determination, reflecting his situation in the 1858 debates of being pitted against the most formidable politician in the nation, and with a moral message that had not yet been embraced by a majority of voters. But what catches my eye in this admirable likeness is the intensity of Lincoln's gaze. The more I see it, the more it evokes a kind of vision that is focused not so much on the here and now as on the future. It is a reminder of something his law partner William H. Herndon called attention to—the aspect of Lincoln's distinctive intellect that made him "long-headed," that is, a person always trying to discern what lies ahead.

Douglas L. Wilson

Abraham Lincoln at Knox College
Avard Fairbanks
October 6, 1958

East Entrance
Old Main
Knox College
Galesburg, Illinois

The Borglum bust of Lincoln appears to keep an unobtrusive watch over an array of college events in Knox College's Lincoln Room. Lincoln seems to gaze across the room toward a large rendering of Victor Perard's sketch of the Fifth Lincoln-Douglas Debate at the College's Old Main on October 7, 1858, for *McClure's Magazine*. Probably because of my relationships with Knox as a graduate and now an employee, I wonder if Lincoln remembered when he debated Douglas that twenty years before he had voted to award the College a charter. Or, did Lincoln expect that Knox would award him an honorary degree two years later? Could Lincoln have foreseen, as then Senator Barack Obama mused shortly after he was awarded an honorary degree by the College in 2005, that the arguments that Lincoln advanced at Knox in 1858 would pave the way for Obama to be elected to the Senate seat that Lincoln lost and then the Presidency that Lincoln also won?

Roger L. Taylor

Lincoln Bust
Gutzon Borglum
1930

Lincoln Room
Knox College
Galesburg, Illinois

Looking at the statue, I see local Lincoln history, no longer buried in dusty old newspaper files and county history books, but engraved in granite on the monument's beautiful plaza.

I feel proud no tax money was used! Once this unique "lost history" was brought forth, our citizens, with contributions, many small and some large, built this tribute so future generations would know and be inspired by their connection to this greatest of all presidents, who:

> As a young circuit riding attorney in 1840 opposed Stephen Douglas to win Livingston County's very first court case … later that day debated him on issues of the day … tended cases here involving meat stealing, slander, adultery …
>
> In February 1855, was made welcome for many days in a Pontiac home after being rescued by sled from a snowbound train miles north of Pontiac, protected from intense cold and strong winds "by blankets from the beds of the citizens of Pontiac."
>
> Spoke to a young men's group in Pontiac on January 27, 1860, and later that evening at a friend's home, had his height marked in a doorway, and speaking of the upcoming convention, predicted he might be picked for the vice presidency, but nothing higher.

Barbara Sancken

Lincoln at Leisure
Rick Harney
June 23, 2006

Livingston County Courthouse
Pontiac, Illinois

Lincoln's last client at the Woodford County Courthouse in Metamora in 1857 was a seventy-year-old woman accused of murdering her abusive seventy-seven-year-old husband. Rather than granting a continuance, the judge gave Lincoln only a recess to prepare a defense for a woman this town didn't want to try, let alone hang. This statue of Lincoln will be joined by another of his client, Melissa Goings, and will depict their last conversation as they walked in the village square – a place he knew well, where he pitched horseshoes and gave legal advice during the years he rode the 8th Judicial Circuit.

Goings escaped before trial, and Abe was actually accused of helping her. The quick-witted Lincoln defused the situation with humor by saying, "I did not chase her off. She simply asked me where she could get a good drink of water, and I said... 'Tennessee has mighty fine drinkin' water!'"

Looking at this statue, I wonder when the future President Lincoln's ability and determination could have been honed, if not during his circuit-riding years, taking on just about any case that came his way and thinking on his feet within a system that was not always as compassionate as he.

Jean Myers

Out of Court
John W. McClarey
To be dedicated in 2009

Metamora Courthouse
Metamora, Illinois

Abraham Lincoln's entrée into the national political arena came about long before his famous debates with Stephen Douglas. From 1847 to 1849, Lincoln served a single term in the United States House of Representatives on behalf of the people of the 7th Congressional District of Illinois. Lincoln's eleven-county district stretched largely in a north-south fashion along the east bank of the Illinois River. From Putnam County on the north end to Scott County on the south end, Lincoln represented a mostly rural district which included the State's capital city of Springfield. It is the very same area I had the privilege to represent in Congress for fourteen years.

Two major national issues which Lincoln confronted upon his arrival on Capitol Hill served as a sentinel call for the future of this son of the prairie. While the battles of the Mexican War were over, the terms of peace were still being debated. Yet, when he arrived in Washington, Lincoln asked whether the war passed constitutional muster and he introduced a resolution demanding to know the exact spot of initial hostilities. The other issue Lincoln addressed was slavery, an issue tied to the Mexican War because of questions about whether slaves would be allowed in the territory ceded to the U.S. at the end of the war. Addressing this issue, Lincoln introduced a resolution which sought to abolish slavery in the District of Columbia.

With his experience in the national legislature behind him, Lincoln headed back to Springfield to work on his law practice. In 1854, though, Lincoln called upon his federal experience to speak out against the Kansas-Nebraska Act authored by Senator Douglas. On October 16 of that year, Lincoln made a triumphal return to the political landscape with his speech in Peoria, outlining his opposition to the legislation and laying the groundwork for his future political successes.

Ray LaHood

Lincoln Draws the Line
John W. McClarey
October 14, 2001

Plaza
Peoria County Courthouse
Peoria, Illinois

This elevated bronze bust is identical to the much better known versions at Lincoln's Tomb in Springfield and the U. S. Capitol Rotunda in Washington. It sits on a tall pedestal in the quiet village of Peoria Heights, Illinois. Most visitors to Tower Park come for the playground or the observation tower, and will see the sculpture only by chance. On its base is a thirty-eight-word sentence taken from Lincoln's well-known 1854 speech in Peoria. Its point about self-government is sound, but his syntax was atypically awkward in this excerpt.

The statue's solitude invites contemplation, as does sculptor Gutzon Borglum's familiar rendering of a pre-presidential Lincoln. The visage is enigmatic, or as he described it, "half smile, half-sadness, half-anger, half forgiveness, half determination, half pause." Despite, or perhaps because of that puzzling look, both Robert T. Lincoln and Theodore Roosevelt admired its authenticity.

Either the park's adjacent observation tower or a short walk along Grandview Drive will give a visitor one of the state's most impressive natural vistas, a sweeping view of the Illinois River valley in its wandering course to the northeast.

Cullom Davis

Bust of Lincoln
Gutzon Borglum
September 20, 1970

Tower Park
Peoria Heights, Illinois

My grandfather Adlai I, a student at Illinois Wesleyan in 1854, recorded grandfather Jesse Fell proposing to Senator Stephen A. Douglas a "joint discussion" of slavery in the territories with a lawyer legislator named Abraham Lincoln. (Lincoln was a member of the state legislature when he first studied law and met Fell.) Douglas declined "with much feeling." But when Mr. Lincoln appeared, the greeting between them was "most cordial—and of the most agreeable and familiar character." The seven debates which followed were each three hours long and attended by thousands drawn on foot, horseback, and in wagons. They brought Lincoln the national attention Fell intended. He then persuaded Lincoln to write his one-page autobiography which Fell employed to promote Lincoln for president. With David Davis, Fell organized the Illinois delegation to the 1860 Republican convention, which reportedly swelled the population of Chicago by forty percent. Thusly did the obscure circuit lawyer legislator become the martyred president, and thusly did America once choose great presidents.

Adlai E. Stevenson III

A. Lincoln the Circuit Lawyer
Keith Knoblock
August 28, 1977

McLean County Law and Justice Center
Bloomington, Illinois

Mr. Lincoln:

It is good to see you back in Bloomington, lounging on the site of the courthouse where you spent so much time over the twenty-three years you regularly came to Bloomington. I have to admit I didn't recognize you at first because of the beard, but the long build and casual air gave you away.

Even though all your local close friends and supporters are gone—David Davis, Jesse Fell, Asahel Gridley, and Leonard Swett to name a few—people still stop by frequently to sit with you.

Your casual relaxed pose still invites people to join you, which was your manner all those times you were here, so involved with law business, politics, and simply friendship.

As the *Daily Pantagraph,* still published here, said on April 18, 1865:

> *Mr. Lincoln has been so well known personally by so large a number of our people, and has so long been regarded as one of our own citizens, that his death seemed to fall with the most crushing severity upon our inhabitants.*

Guy Fraker

The Lincoln Bench
Rick Harney
July 2000

McLean County Museum of History
Bloomington, Illinois

It's not known if, when, or if ever, Abraham Lincoln, Jesse Fell, and David Davis met and took a walk. But here they are strolling, engaged in conversation every viewer will construct for themselves.

The three were old Whigs, members of a failed political party who were anxiously trying to build a new party—one that would link the ideas of building wealth with stopping the expansion of slavery. Fell came into Bloomington with a satchel of books and a head full of ideas. He convinced David Davis to come here as well, selling him his law business and a home place that Davis was to improve over the years. Davis was interested in improving a lot of things. Some say Lincoln was his biggest project.

Lincoln was the odd man out here. He had none of Fell's Quaker quietude and polish; none of Davis's ease and tidewater charm. Yet here Lincoln is listening, being cajoled perhaps, for Fell was to suggest strongly that he run for the presidency, and publish his autobiography, and Davis was to manage Lincoln's nomination at the Republican convention of 1860, though he had to wait two years for a thank you—a seat on the U.S. Supreme Court.

Greg Koos

Lincoln, Fell, and Davis in Bloomington
Andrew Jumonville
Maquette
To be dedictated in 2009

Bloomington Center for the Performing Arts
Bloomington, Illinois

Standing in early fall at this crossroads bounding Logan and Tazewell Counties, with one foot in each, the horizon is the predominant reference punctuating this vertical marker. The horse prints and wagon wheel tracks of the original trace on Delavan Road have long been erased and paved over from memory, but even a few miles off Route 136 one can lose one's orientation to the surrounding, endless horizon.

Tazewell County, established in 1827, was carved out of the larger tract including Peoria and was named for Littleton Tazewell, senator and later governor of the state of Virginia. Logan County was created by a bill sponsored by Abraham Lincoln in 1839, and was more appropriately named for an Illinois physician, Dr. John Logan, whose son became a famous Civil War General.

I squint into the western sky, feel the early cool coming on, geese flying south, the corn rustling, ready for harvest, and I can imagine the tallgrass prairie stretching out uninterrupted for miles. My great-great-grandfather might have seen it this way in the 1830s, when he first arrived from Connecticut, or my great-grandfather in the 1860s. Both befriended Abraham Lincoln as he rode the "circuit" north from Springfield where he watered his horse at the bottom of their Elkhart Hill farm on his way to Postville, which later became the Logan County seat of Lincoln and was christened ceremoniously by the not-yet president in 1853 with the juice of a watermelon. Local lore has it that the blocks of the town are uneven because they were paced off by the long-legged Lincoln in one direction and my shorter great- grandfather in the other.

William M. Drake

Lincoln Circuit Marker
Edgar D. Martin, Design
Joseph Dux, Plaque
1922

Logan-Tazewell County Line
Near Emden, Illinois

In some respects, *Abraham Lincoln, the Student* at Lincoln College captures an unfamiliar Lincoln. Sculpted specifically for the college in 1961 by artist Merrell Gage, in this statue we see a simple young Lincoln with an open book on his lap. Absent are the dignified clothes and the familiar beard and top hat. It is without the stony determination and deity-like presence witnessed at the Lincoln Memorial.

Yet devoid of these elements, *Abraham Lincoln, the Student* remains characteristically Abraham Lincoln, and quintessentially very American. Here is the self-taught Abraham Lincoln, who rose from humble origins, and whose accomplishments catapulted him into the annals of American memory. Well established is Lincoln's unquenchable absorption in books. Lincoln recognized the imperative of education, and noted in his first political campaign speech in 1832 that it is "the most important subject which we as a people can be engaged in." Similarly, this statue bears his quotation: "I shall prepare myself. One day my chance will come." This phrase should serve as the mantra for us all.

But it is more than mere learning. Within that Lincoln maxim is composed the enduring American dream: through preparation and ambition may one realize his full potential, limited only by self-imposed restraints. Education allowed Lincoln to grasp the mantle of leadership, and allowed him to persevere through the battles of the Civil War, the battles from his many opponents, and the battles within himself. Lincoln is testament that a ready, open mind makes possible human progress, cultivating new paths hitherto unexplored.

Abraham Lincoln, the Student affords a familiar Lincoln after all. This statue beckons us to imitate the greatness found in Lincoln. It compels us to improve ourselves and our world, to constantly prepare and remake ourselves to fit our larger dreams. May this sculpture awaken the student in each of us.

Ron J. Keller

Abraham Lincoln, the Student
Robert Merrell Gage
May 28, 1961

Lincoln College
Lincoln, Illinois

As Abraham Lincoln transitioned out of his statehouse headquarters in late December of 1860, the sculptor Thomas Jones, who was commissioned to model a bust of Lincoln, set up a provisional studio in the nearby St. Nicholas Hotel. Jones carefully observed Lincoln during the seven-week period between his arrival in Springfield and the president-elect's farewell. In *Abraham Lincoln and Others at the St. Nicholas,* Wayne Temple notes that Jones and Lincoln met outside of the hotel at Cook's Hall on the evening of January 8, 1861. They were there to enjoy a performance of Shakespeare's *Hamlet* by James Murdoch, an accomplished actor. Imagine Lincoln's face, at once at ease and in thought, as he watched and listened to Murdoch. Imagine Jones as he turned his attention from the performer to the president-elect and discovered another perspective of the character behind Lincoln's countenance. Although we will never know exactly when Jones captured in clay the slight form of Lincoln's smile and the brilliant gaze of his eyes, the features of this classic bust appear to connect to that cold night in January of 1861, when the artist and the politician took in these words:

To be, or not to be—that is the question:
Whether 'tis nobler in the mind to suffer
The slings and arrows of outrageous fortune,
Or to take arms against a sea of troubles,
And by opposing end them.

Justin A. Blandford

Lincoln the President
Thomas Dow Jones
January 1861

Lincoln Heritage Museum
Lincoln College
Lincoln, Illinois

This life-size statue of Abraham Lincoln was presented on June 21, 1939, to the citizens of Logan County by the local Kiwanis and Rotary clubs. The *Lincoln Evening Courier* reported that the six-feet, four-inches work was a duplicate of a Saint-Gaudens statue of Lincoln in Lincoln Park in Chicago. Sculptor Max Bachmann depicted a beardless Lincoln as he would have been known to Central Illinois during his circuit-riding days. A Logan County judge and historian, Lawrence B. Stringer, delivered the acceptance address.

My own memories of the statue in our courthouse come from trips with my father when he had business in that imposing building. In those days, the statue was white. Only recently was it painted to look life-like.

As a boy, looking at the statue reminded me of family stories about my great-grandfather, James Beaver, who came to Logan County in the spring of 1853 and established our family farm. Local histories reveal that James Beaver joined the "new" Republican party and became a strong supporter of Abraham Lincoln.

Paul J. Beaver

Abraham Lincoln
Compilation by P. P. Caproni & Bro.
Body: Augustus Saint-Gaudens, *Lincoln the Man*, Lincoln Park, Chicago, Illinois
Head: Max Bachmann
June 21, 1939

Logan County Courthouse
Lincoln, Illinois

Abraham Lincoln was the attorney for the Chicago and Mississippi Railroad. On February 14, 1853, Colby Knapp, a member of the Illinois State Legislature, introduced a bill (drafted by Abraham Lincoln) that established the completion of the railroad from Alton to Chicago. Lands along the right-of-way would increase in value. The steam engines of the day needed to replenish water for the thirsty boilers at a maximum of thirty-mile intervals, establishing "jerkwater" facilities along the route. Postville was about thirty miles equidistant from Springfield and Bloomington. Postville had a future! But the "new" town needed a new name.

Three men, all known to Lincoln ... a Springfield neighbor, a director of the railroad, and the Sheriff of Logan County ... became interested in a joint business venture and needed legal assistance to establish their "Town Site Company." Abraham Lincoln was chosen. Lincoln's exceptional contribution to the success of the project prompted the business partners later to resolve to call their new town "LINCOLN."

On August 27, 1853, at the outdoor opening of the sale for building lots, Lincoln was asked to "christen" his namesake town site. Obligingly Lincoln selected a water- melon from a wagon on the site. With his pocket knife he opened the melon, squeezing water from the core into a tin cup. His "christening" words as he poured the water from the tin cup to the ground concluded with the announcement that the new town "LINCOLN" would soon be named the permanent county seat of Logan County. And it was.

Today, in the atrium of the State Bank of Lincoln, in Lincoln, Illinois (within a few hundred feet of the original christening site), on a pedestal, stands the bigger than life-size sculpture of a tall, lean figure of a circuit-riding lawyer, an inverted tin cup in his right hand and at his feet spillage and a broken watermelon.

Earl W. Henderson, Jr.

The Ages of Lincoln
Edna Goodenough
1970

State Bank of Lincoln
111 N. Sangamon Street
Lincoln, Illinois

This remarkable tribute to Lincoln which stands on Route 66 in Lincoln, Illinois, was created by David Bentley. Bentley is a life-long resident of Illinois, a twenty-eight-year veteran of law enforcement, and a man with a passion for Lincoln. He decided to express that passion in something big—very big. So he created a wagon and a Lincoln that together stand twenty-four feet tall and weigh five tons. Exercising the prerogative of an artist, he chose symbolism over historical exactness. His Lincoln is riding in a Conestoga wagon to signify the prairie years; he's reading a law book and sporting a very presidential beard. The sheer size alone is an expression of the iconic figure that has now become larger-than-life. Admittedly, some Lincoln aficionados, accustomed to a more formal reverential rendering of Lincoln, might find this interpretation slightly disconcerting, but I have to believe that if Lincoln happened to be traveling down Route 66 and came upon this likeness, he would probably get a darn good chuckle out of it.

Nicky Stratton

The Railsplitter Covered Wagon
David Bentley
November 2001

Corner of Woodlawn Road and Route 66
Lincoln, Illinois

Abraham Lincoln stands silently looking over the Clinton town square. However, the words inscribed on the base share powerful messages. Whether he said the famous words ("You can fool all of the people some of the time and some of the people all of the time, but you can't fool all of the people all of the time") matters not. The words are true and timeless. There are other important words on the base ("Stand with anybody that stands right. Stand with him while he is right and part with him when he goes wrong.").

While Lincoln stands silently, I can hear him utter profound words. I hear the Gettysburg Address. I hear the Second Inaugural. I hear the House Divided Speech. I hear colorful jokes. I hear debates with political opponents. I hear arguments before a jury. I hear Abraham Lincoln.

John A. Lupton

Abraham Lincoln
Albert L. Van den Berghen
November 11, 1931

Mr. Lincoln's Square Park
Clinton, Illinois

Standing there in Carle Park, *Lincoln the Lawyer* might be leaning back against the rail of a jury box, surveying a courtroom. If his client in this imaginary case is a railroad, as some of his clients actually were, so much the better, because this statue is, after all, in the Twin Cities.

Champaign blossomed on the prairie adjacent to Urbana because of a dispute—about land, of course—with the Illinois Central. Lincoln, the archetypical American, was an active participant in the nineteenth-century's tumultuous unleashing of the commercial energies that made modern America, and made it not a moment too soon: The North's industrialism, and the Union forces' uses of railroads, helped preserve the nation.

Yes, before Lincoln was president, he was a lawyer, and as president he remained one. With his first words uttered as president—his long (it is five times as long as his Second Inaugural) and sinewy First Inaugural Address—he made himself the nation's lawyer-in-chief. To read that closely reasoned argument, made just thirty-nine days before the firing on Fort Sumter, is, in a sense, to read the most important legal brief ever submitted in America.

It was submitted not to an actual court but to the court of public opinion. The fact that the case Lincoln made—about his duties as chief executive, and against the legality of secession—was settled by the sword does not diminish the nobility of his insistence that legalities should be clearly understood before the sword was unsheathed. Hence the durable dignity of the statue, and the fact, of *Lincoln the Lawyer*.

George Will

Lincoln the Lawyer
Lorado Taft
July 3, 1927

Carle Park
Urbana, Illinois

This bust of Lincoln stands at the east quadrangle entrance to Lincoln Hall. It is the cornerstone building of public higher education in the State of Illinois, opened in 1913. The bust is accessible to students and, apparently, friendly since Lincoln's nose is shiny from the passing touch of thousands of students over many years. I liked seeing this.

Lincoln's most enduring leadership contributions were, of course, preserving the unity of the United States by winning the Civil War and ending slavery. But close behind, in my opinion, was signing the Morrill Act of 1862 that created America's land grant universities. Their purpose was to build a strong democracy and a strong economy while enabling individuals to achieve their dreams through a nearly free college education for ordinary people with the intelligence and drive to succeed. This purpose has been, and continues to be, brilliantly achieved.

Today, Lincoln Hall awaits a much-needed renovation and modernization after nearly a century of hard use. I decided after visiting the Lincoln bust in the entry way that if Lincoln could preserve the Union, end slavery, and launch land grant institutions during his presidency, my colleagues and I in the leadership of the University of Illinois and the State of Illinois must preserve and perpetuate his legacy by, among other things, taking proper care of Lincoln Hall and our great University.

And we will.

B. Joseph White

Lincoln Bust
Hermon Atkins MacNeil
Before 1928

Lincoln Hall
University of Illinois
Urbana, Illinois

A young, beardless, thoughtful-appearing Lincoln gazes at a child's playground in Champaign, Illinois's West Side Park. Overlooking the playground, the raised concrete and bronze plaque monolith represents Lincoln as a young lawyer during the early years of his circuit-riding career. It is clearly a mid-twentieth-century style representation that suggests the rugged frontiersman-turned-lawyer. The rugged surface connotes a no-nonsense, earnest lawyer, suggesting nothing of the ribald humor with which he entertained his peers on the circuit. On the other hand, one can imagine this Lincoln using homespun and earthy examples to sway the frontiersmen listening in the jury box as Lincoln defends one of the many defendants who sought his help over the years.

Nearby in the park, one will find a three-piece sculpture garden designed by the same sculptor, in the same style, depicting two frontier boys, a horse, and a dog. One can easily imagine a young Lincoln interacting with the boys as he rests from his legal responsibilities.

The monolith is nineteen feet high and six feet wide. Although the plaque has been cleaned and sealed, the concrete is weathered and shows signs of abuse. It originally stood in downtown Champaign, but in recent years was removed and placed in West Side Park.

Roger D. Bridges

Lincoln Memorial
William Fothergill
Circa 1966

West Side Park
Champaign, Illinois

Bachmann's bust of Lincoln portrays eyes looking outward and upward. This is a man calling for "our better angels," for "malice toward none; with charity for all." Perhaps Lincoln is searching the distant future and hoping for a land of equal rights and equal opportunity as proposed in his beloved Declaration of Independence. At first glance, the bust exudes a strength of character, a powerful, almost austere, authority. A closer examination reveals more. The strength is framed in a gentle kindness about the face, a quiet, resolved dignity. It is very much like Lincoln the man. Lincoln was that rare person who manifested seemingly contradictory characteristics; we can see his charisma as well as his humility, his firmness as well as his compassion. And he instinctively knew the appropriate time to be tough or tender; and that eclecticism contributed to his greatness! Our family has long enjoyed Bachmann's rendition of Lincoln; the people of Urbana are fortunate to have this bust in their library and are fortunate to have Lincoln as one of their forebears in our Land of Lincoln.

Orville Vernon Burton

Bust of Abraham Lincoln
Max Bachmann
Circa 1915

The Urbana Free Library
210 West Green Street
Urbana, Illinois

The Quincy plaque was the last of my grandfather's works. He was an Illinois native, and most of his sculptures reflect American themes—Washington, Black Hawk, pioneers, Grant, and, of course, Lincoln. He and my grandmother read aloud from the Sandburg chapters on the Lincoln-Douglas debates over the extension of slavery. It has an apt description of Lincoln by a visitor in Quincy: "No one could doubt that the cause for which he was speaking was the only thing he had at heart. He was the representative of an idea. His great strength was in his trusting the people instead of considering them as babes in arms ... I never saw a more thoughtful face. I never saw a more dignified face. I never saw so sad a face."

Jean Taft Douglas Bandler

Lincoln-Douglas Debate Memorial Relief
Lorado Taft
October 13, 1936

Washington Park
Quincy, Illinois

Entering the political arena takes courage, a willingness to stand before public opinion and risk the condemnation or even contempt of neighbors and friends, those whose opinions we value most. Yet Abraham Lincoln possessed what Ernest Hemingway later saluted as the highest degree of courage, grace under pressure. Throughout his lengthy political career, Lincoln fearlessly confronted that which he deemed a threat to the republic, to the law, and to the Constitution. He condemned a sitting president for maneuvering his country into what he regarded as an unjust war, heedless of the fact that the conflict was quite popular with his constituents. He debated and ultimately bested the pugnacious and talented stump speaker, Stephen A. Douglas, widely acknowledged at the time as the foremost political figure in the United States. At Cooper Union, Lincoln faced down the howling rage of the slave power and urged the fledgling Republican Party and indeed all American citizens to stand firm against the expansion of slavery, to have faith that right makes might, to follow the path of duty whatever the opposition. Abraham Lincoln's political life is a paean to courage against innumerable obstacles, and in the end, Lincoln's triumph marked victory for what Frederick Douglass called the "saving principles" of the Declaration of Independence.

R. Dan Monroe

Abraham Lincoln's First Political Speech
Anthony Vestuto
October 12, 1968

Lincoln Square
Decatur, Illinois

Boris Lovet-Lorski, 1894-1973, a sculptor of international prominence, was born in Lithuania. His larger-than-life bronze of *Lincoln the Young Lawyer* in Decatur, Illinois, exaggerates certain proportions of the Lincoln physique, like the length of the neck and size of the hands, perhaps to make a point. The large hands suggest to me a quality of character in the Lincoln persona like strength of purpose. The right hand is extended forward as though making an appeal for justice and fairness to his client. The statue brings to mind Lincoln's practice at the old Macon County Courthouse in the period 1837-38 and in the county's second courthouse that was constructed in 1839. The present courthouse, constructed in 1939, is a fitting backdrop to connect Lincoln as a traveling circuit rider in the Illinois 8th Judicial Circuit before his rise as a national leader.

More importantly, the statue represents Lincoln at his best in that he often appealed to his fellow citizens to show the "better angels of our nature," a practice that became part of the Lincoln persona as a private citizen and as a public figure. His lifetime practice of kindliness was first learned as a boy from his parents. This character trait transformed him and the nation as it was expressed through acts of kindness to animals as well as to humans, to children, to friend and foe alike, to political rivals, to troublesome members of his cabinet and administration, to the disenfranchised, to the bondsman, to the captive, to those falsely accused before the courts, to the widow and her orphan, to old friends of bygone days, to wounded soldiers, to those who had borne the brunt of battle, and finally to defeated Southerners at the end of the Civil War. The Lovet-Lorski statue of Lincoln at its best represents us, the heirs of the Lincoln legacy.

John W. McClarey

Lincoln the Young Lawyer
Boris Lovet-Lorski
September 8, 1946

Macon County Courthouse
Decatur, Illinois

Lincoln at Millikin University

You know, this was all hardwood forest, red oak
pin oak, shingle oak, boxwood, and shagbark
hickory—and I cut through it with an oversized axe
as sharp as my legal arguments on the old
Eighth Circuit. Yes, I was sleeping that day
when they nominated me for the Presidency,
about a half-mile due east of here, May tenth,
eighteen sixty. I delivered my first speech here,
back in the summer of eighteen thirty, exhorting
the locals to improve the old Sangamon River,
which is still flowing south of here, now clogged
with old shoes, tin cans, and the odd beer bottle.
On winter mornings, I'm wide awake, wearing a cap
of snow, icicles dangling from the bulbous tip of my
metallic nose. Blue jays, sparrows, and chickadees
land on my bronze back: I guess I've become the genius
of the place, guardian angel, resident divinity, and part-
time student, picking up a little Spanish, some English
Literature and a little bit of Wittgenstein from faculty
and students gathered at my feet, for whom I am
the frozen figure in bronze, dead as history, when
all the time I am listening, and very much alive.

Daniel Guillory

At Twenty-One I Came to Illinois
Fred M. Torrey
October 24, 1948

Millikin University
Decatur, Illinois

It was a summer's day in 1972.

We had come to her favorite spot, a grassy prairie, site of Abraham Lincoln's cabin overlooking the Sangamon River west of Decatur, Illinois.

My Mother was seventy-two and for her this place solidified who she was, where she had been, and what she had become.

Ella Simons was the second-oldest of thirteen siblings, born to a coal miner in 1899. She attended grade school in Monica, Illinois, and chose piano lessons over a formal education. This decision would have a profound effect on how she would raise her two daughters.

As a young woman she lived and worked for a farm couple. Her husband-to-be, a widowed chicken farmer with three children, hired her to be his housekeeper. She bore five children, two of whom died in miscarriages, and a third of whooping cough. Out of the pain and despair, she divorced and set out to protect and provide for her two daughters in 1936.

For the next twenty-five years she did menial labor and deprived herself of any personal comfort. In the 1950s Mary Ann graduated from Bradley University with a Performance Degree in Music, and Katherine from Millikin University with a Bachelor of Science Degree.

She could now rest for she had been the instrument through which her legacy would live on through her daughters.

As I view the statue, I know that she identified herself with him—Abraham Lincoln had been her silent mentor.

Carl Sandburg describes Lincoln in *The Prairie Years* as possessing noble traits, honesty, a compassion for the underdog, a clear-sighted vision of right and wrong, a dedication to God and Country, and an abiding concern for all.

Among her modest possessions was a picture of Lincoln, a bronze statue acquired on a trip to Springfield, Illinois, and eight volumes of Abraham Lincoln's papers read from cover to cover.

She was and I am.................her daughter.

Katherine Simons Kowa

Vision for a Greater Illinois
John W. McClarey
September 4, 2004

The Macon County Historical Museum and Prairie Village
5580 North Fork Road
Decatur, Illinois

Almost anyone who would apply the "Lincoln Rorschach test" to this statue would assume that it is the work of a single sculptor. In fact, it is not. The statue juxtaposes a head of Lincoln, modeled in 1905 by Max Bachmann (1862-1921), an obscure German-born sculptor, on a body based on the *Lincoln the Man*, completed in 1887 by Augustus Saint-Gaudens (1848-1907), the leading American sculptor of his generation.

Body and head were brought together by P. P. Caproni and Bro., a Boston partnership formed in 1892, which, with or without permission, cast reproductions of thousands of ancient, medieval, and modern sculptures for schools, libraries, museums, theaters, and "private connoisseurs" across the land. The sculptor Lorado Taft saluted the "beauty" that the Caproni firm "brought into American schools and homes" through its reproductions (which included Taft's own Columbus, Black Hawk, and Lincoln). "When I am in Boston," he wrote in 1933, "I generally visit the Museum of Art; I always go to the Caproni shops."

Pietro and Emilio Caproni, enterprising Italian immigrants, first sold Bachmann's Lincoln with and without a beard, in 1905. In 1909, their *Lincoln in Sculpture* circular offered nine other Lincoln pieces. By 1911, they had placed Bachmann's head on the shoulders of their own rendition of Saint-Gaudens's body. They sold copies of this hybrid Lincoln as late as 1939, and collectors may still buy the Bachmann bust from a successor firm. Even in 2007, the 1930 bronze copy of the statue on a parkway in Minneapolis was restored and rededicated.

Today, the *Macon County History Museum Lincoln*, which once stood in Decatur's Lincoln Grade School, solemnly looks down on visiting school children. The seven-foot, two-inch statue dominates them and their surroundings, which include the American flag, a painting by a regional artist, and a picture of John W. McClarey's Lincoln statue outside the building. Thus they experience Lincoln's commanding presence in the American pantheon.

John Hoffmann

Macon County History Museum Lincoln
Composite by P. P. Caproni & Bro.
Head: Max Bachmann
Body: After Augustus Saint-Gaudens, *Lincoln the Man,* Lincoln Park, Chicago, Illinois
1911

The Macon County History Museum and Prairie Village
5580 North Fork Road
Decatur, Illinois

Troosting in Decatur is certainly one of the more unusual Lincoln sculptures. No marble, no pedestal, no foreboding presence of the sixteenth president. He is flat on his back, being carried by two other men. Looks like a fraternity prank at a football game or "mosh pit" at a rock concert.

But what is depicted here is actually what happened at the Illinois State Republican Convention in Decatur on May 8, 1860 (shortly before the national convention that nominated Lincoln for the presidency).

The convention was held in a building that could hold nine hundred. In fact, three thousand rambunctious Republicans filled the hall, with Lincoln trying to remain inconspicuous amongst them. When chairman of the convention and Lincoln supporter Richard Oglesby announced Lincoln's presence in the hall, the throng cheered, but Lincoln could not make his way to the speaker's platform because of the multitude. Since Lincoln could not go through the crowd, he went over the crowd, being passed from Republican to Republican to the front. This convention was where "Honest Abe" and "The Railsplitter" labels were first applied to Lincoln by Oglesby. The labels had power and have endured to this day.

How did Lincoln make it to the pinnacle of power? He was helped every step along the way by his friends, his supporters, and his family. That is what the sculpture conveys to us. Two anonymous men, working to advance Lincoln to the top. They did their part. So did David Davis, Richard Oglesby, Jesse Fell, Leonard Swett, and all the other citizens who knew that Lincoln was the man to be our president.

Mary F. and William G. Shepherd

Troosting
John W. McClarey
2008

130 North Water Street
South of Central Park
Decatur, Illinois

In 1908, a life-sized bronze silhouette, or bas relief, was created by John McClarey. Best known as *Barnwell's Lincoln,* its origin is in a photo captured by Edward Barnwell, who desired to take a picture of "the biggest man" at the 1860 Illinois State Republican Convention. Subsequently, Lincoln posed for the picture and was nominated for president.

At first glance, the silhouette speaks to the qualities of strength, courage, and determination. However, a closer view dramatizes Lincoln as the wise, sensitive, humbled, and troubled Lincoln whose image rests in our hearts today.

Although the silhouette reflects realistic details in Lincoln's buttons, boots, and necktie, more subtle implications shine through in his gaunt face, sad eyes, and pensive facial expression. I see him deep in thought as he ponders a strategy which will provide the gift of freedom for our nation and future generations.

In *Barnwell's Lincoln* I see a little of ourselves when faced with insurmountable challenges. It inspires us to become problem solvers of our own destiny.

As we celebrate Lincoln's Bicentennial, the sculpture helps us honor and commemorate his 200th Birthday by remembering that without Lincoln there would not be the United States of America we cherish today.

Marilyn Kushak

Barnwell's Lincoln
John W. McClarey
2008

130 North Water Street
South of Central Park
Decatur, Illinois

Like all statues of Lincoln, *On the Circuit* is a kind of commentary. It tells us what the sculptor, and his audience, thought about the man they were honoring. At first look *On the Circuit* suggests Lincoln's gentleness: the horse dawdles but the master is too kind to prod him. The animal is so big it might have been a plow horse, busting the sod of Central Illinois. Instead it's been enlisted to carry a young lawyer on the legal circuit from county courthouse to county courthouse. The scene is rustic, but it holds the promise of something more—a way of living beyond the hardscrabble life of physical toil that Lincoln was born into. And the way there, the way out, is through the book Lincoln holds in his hand. It absorbs him so completely he seems lost to the world that surrounds him, the world of knotted trees and split-rail fences and ploughed-up fields. Anna Hyatt Huntington used Lincoln to show the triumph of modernism: the victory of the life of the mind over a life of grunt work, of brains over muscle, and she was showing, through the open law book, how the victory was won.

Andrew Ferguson

On the Circuit
Anna Vaughn Hyatt Huntington
1963

Lincoln's New Salem
New Salem, Illinois

"I am humble Abraham Lincoln." That's how he introduced himself in his first campaign speech at New Salem in 1832. He was twenty-three and a new resident of this obscure village in Central Illinois, a place like thousands of others on the frontier. He lived there for six influential years, working as a clerk and a postmaster, and yes, splitting rails and making fences. But also making friends and connections, and constantly seeking to improve himself. Years later, a successful lawyer and influential politician (but not yet president), he outlined his strategy to an aspiring young man. "Get books, and read and study them carefully." At New Salem he was always reading. He taught himself rhetoric with Kirkham's Grammar. He devoured Shakespeare, Milton, and Pope, Gibbon, Byron, and Burns. He became a master of our language, the most eloquent of our statesmen. He turned to the law first as literature, only later as the pathway to a career. "His ambition," his partner William Herndon declared, "was a little engine that knew no rest." He prepares to lay his ax aside, stride out of New Salem into his future, and into our history.

John Mack Faragher

Lincoln at the Crossroads of Decision
Avard Fairbanks
June 21, 1954

Lincoln's New Salem
New Salem, Illinois

Ancient peoples looked with wonder to the stars in the sky, the endless bodies of water, and boundless forests, musing at what might lie beyond. To Abraham Lincoln, that sense of wonder and awe was represented in the wilderness of his youth. He spent twenty-eight years in the wilderness. Both the rifle and ax became symbols of the frontier. Lincoln's adeptness with the ax might provide the foundation for the next great city that he hoped would be New Salem. If nature was something to be tamed, it also remained something of wonder and beauty.

Thomas F. Schwartz

Out of the Wilderness
Marshall Mitchell
May 15, 1992

Lincoln's New Salem
New Salem, Illinois

Abraham Lincoln comes forth here as a confident young man seeking boundaries and directions, and a niche for himself. Lincoln at New Salem was a roustabout, a boatman, a storekeeper, a student of the law, a militiaman, a successful politician, and for four years, he was a surveyor. An exacting pursuit in which Lincoln took pride, surveying taught him some of the discipline that he would later need to succeed as a lawyer, and in his subsequent political career.

Rodney O. Davis

A. Lincoln – Deputy Surveyor, Sangamon County, Illinois 1833-1837
John W. McClarey
October 4, 2003

Lincoln's New Salem
New Salem, Illinois

The Andrew O'Connor statue of Abraham Lincoln was dedicated in 1918, when I was two years old. By the time I was twelve I was allowed to take the streetcar downtown by myself to go to swimming lessons at the YWCA. On my way I liked to stop at the Centennial Museum to see those dioramas of Sangamon Indian life, and a woodsy scene of indigenous mushrooms, the poisonous ones alarmingly marked with red skull and crossbones.

Then I could walk down the block where, in front of the Illinois State Capitol building, I could gaze at the beardless, gangly Lincoln with great admiration. I was embarrassed that my great-grandfather Charles Henry Lanphier had been publisher of the Democratic *Illinois State Register* and was a dedicated supporter of Stephen A. Douglas. I didn't understand that Douglas was in his own right a distinguished man and able opponent of Lincoln, and he well deserves his own statue not far away, near the steps to the Capitol building.

I left Springfield in 1938 to marry a mining engineer. We lived in a variety of places, but for fifty years I have lived in the Boston area. As a docent teaching children at their Museum of Fine Arts, I became very familiar with the five-foot bronze replica of Daniel Chester French's great figure of Lincoln that is in his Memorial in Washington. This Lincoln is bearded, older and wearier as he sits in a contemplative but determined pose. It is an heroic figure, but my thoughts always return to the O'Connor Lincoln whom I first knew.

Now I realize the Springfield figure is positioned on the rear platform of the train at the depot where he is bidding good-bye to old friends and neighbors as he departs for the unknown but certainly difficult responsibilities of the presidency and the looming problems of slavery. His feet are awkwardly placed, his posture is unpretentious, yet the potential for greatness is evident. His words, "Here I have lived," touch me deeply.

Marnie Lanphier Wengren

Candidate
Andrew O'Connor, Jr.
October 15, 1918

Grounds
Illinois State Capitol
Springfield, Illinois

With the possible exception of the magnificent Lincoln Memorial in Washington, D.C., this is my favorite statue of Lincoln. This is Abraham Lincoln by the sculptor who knew him best in the unique role that defines him best: *Emancipator*.

To Lincoln, the Emancipation Proclamation was a matter of "military necessity." With the stroke of his pen, he not only freed four million slaves in seceded states, he also severed a lifeline of the Confederate army. No longer could slaves be forced into military support roles for Confederate troops.

A year later, more than 130,000 former slaves were serving in the Union cause—a validation of the proclamation as a shrewd military strategy.

But the real genius of the Emancipation Proclamation, far more than its military sagacity, is its moral audacity. By insisting on the fundamental right of human liberty, the Emancipation Proclamation transcends time and national borders and remains today a source of hope for freedom-seeking people around the world.

During the years I worked in the Illinois State Capitol, I passed this statue hundreds of times. It was a daily reminder that we can, with great courage, make our highest political ideals a reality. Perhaps a replica should stand in every capitol.

Richard J. Durbin

Emancipator
Leonard Wells Volk
Created 1876 (Placed 1905)

Second Floor Rotunda
Illinois State Capitol
Springfield, Illinois

In the Lincoln-Douglas debates, Stephen A. Douglas accused Abraham Lincoln of being two-faced. Lincoln turned toward his audience and retorted: "If I had two faces, would I be wearing this one?"

Little did he know when he uttered this humorous line that on his 200th birthday, his face would be one of the most recognizable in history.

We at the Illinois Supreme Court are delighted that a bust of this great man would adorn the Great Hall outside our courtroom. Sculptor John McClarey's Lincoln is *The Prairie Lawyer*; not the politician, not the bearded, iconic Emancipator immortalized in marble on the National Mall. The bronze strikes a deliberative, thoughtful pose. It embodies a Lincoln of equanimity and resolve. It is a Lincoln who, we are sure, would follow the admonition we see etched in Latin above the attorney's entry as we sit upon the Bench inside. "Hear the Other Side," it says. In McClarey's rendering, Lincoln is listening.

Lincoln appeared more than 400 times before the Supreme Court when it sat at the Old State Capitol in Springfield.

We all stand in his shadow, and as lawyers in Illinois we are privileged to serve as his colleague. *The Prairie Lawyer* is a visage of decency and fairness, thoughtfulness and strength. It serves as an inspiration to both the members of the Supreme Court and the lawyers who appear before us to accept the lessons garnered from the self-taught attorney who walked the streets outside our building on his way to becoming our 16th President.

Thomas R. Fitzgerald

Prairie Lawyer—Master of Us All
John W. McClarey
January 12, 2009

Great Hall
Illinois Supreme Court Building
Springfield, Illinois

When I look at the Thomas D. Jones bust of Lincoln in the Executive Mansion Library, I am reminded that Lincoln was a frequent visitor to the Mansion where he would sit in the evening with Governor William Bissell. Governor Bissell was a paraplegic who rarely left the Mansion, and Lincoln would assist him with his papers and messages.

James R. Thompson

Lincoln the President
Thomas Dow Jones
January 1861

Library
Executive Mansion
Springfield, Illinois

As a small child my beloved aunt, Elizabeth Brown Ide, frequently took me to visit the Illinois State Museum. There I would stand spellbound before the dioramas. My favorites were the Underground Railroad and the scenes of our native Indian tribes grouped around their campfires.

Recently on a frigid December morning, my husband and I stood outside the museum studying the famous Lincoln totem. The powerful carving of Abraham Lincoln atop the pole seemed a fitting tribute by an Alaskan Indian tribe to the great emancipator's belief in equality and freedom.

Owsley Brown Thunman and N. Ronald Thunman

Proud Raven Totem Pole
Originally carved by Thleda of the Raven Clan of the Tlingit Indians on Tongass Island, Alsaska
Original 1883, Replica 1966

Yard
Illinois State Museum
Springfield, Illinois

Jo Davidson's 1947 Bust of *Abraham Lincoln* imparts a sense of a tough yet humble man who would be somewhat embarrassed by the amount of attention that was focused on him during the Lincoln Bicentennial, and indeed over the last 150 years since the Civil War. An Abraham Lincoln who would deflect such praise and attention away from himself and toward others; to the memories of the soldiers who fought and died in the Civil War; to the African Americans who struggled in slavery with the hope of freedom; and, to all those who continue to dream of the freedom to rise as far as their abilities and ambition will take them.

There is something else there, a slight grin, as though he is enjoying the activity in the Lincoln Home National Historic Site visitor center where the statue is on display and where countless families and school groups begin their visit to the Springfield home where Lincoln raised his family. Perhaps Lincoln is also smiling at the antics of the children, their laughter and occasional prank between school classmates that might remind us all of two other Lincolns, young Willie and Tad, who so often brought joy into their father's life.

Timothy P. Townsend

Bust of Abraham Lincoln
Jo Davidson
1947

Visitor Center
Lincoln Home National Historic Site
Springfield, Illinois

In a city that holds the distinction of having more than a dozen realistic and heroic statues of Abraham Lincoln by such renowned sculptors as Andrew O'Connor, Larkin Mead, Leonard Volk, Fred Torrey, Gutzon Borglum, and John McClarey, Abbott Pattison's *Abstract Lincoln* "sticks out like a sore thumb." Controversial from the day it was unveiled at the Capitol Avenue entrance to Lincoln Library, the Public Library of Springfield, on November 21, 1976, the statue remains the butt of many jokes.

During a press interview, Pattison admitted that it was difficult to design his Lincoln for a building in a city filled with traditional and classical portrayals of our sixteenth president. He said it was as if he were walking a tightrope, "straddling a resemblance, something to do with Lincoln, with being sympathetic to the lines and shape of the building."

When I look at *Abstract Lincoln*, I see the work of an artist who created a statue exactly the way he conceptualized it. I see a president who is lonely and grappling with the problems of saving the Union. I see a leader agonizing over the tremendous loss of life on both sides of the Civil War.

Carl Volkmann

Abstract Lincoln
Abbott Lawrence Pattison
November 21, 1976

Lincoln Library, the Public Library of Springfield
Springfield, Illinois

When you're the mayor's son, sometimes you need to disappear for an hour or more. Leland Woods was good; the old Lincoln Library even better. Both my 1950s refuges are now gone, but I loved the freedom and privacy of that gray limestone building at the corner of Seventh and Capitol. Like so many Carnegie libraries, its Beaux-Arts plan was solid and dignified—two stories high, two wings wide—yet up in its stacks, the glass-block floors and wrought-iron shelves made book-hunting and reading into adventure. When I looked up from bound volumes of *Harper's* or *Collier's*, I felt like an explorer in a softly lit ice cave.

On an outside balcony, above the entrance door, stood a bust of the library's namesake. Coming or going, I sent Mr. Lincoln a nod, in private thanks for the privilege of growing up in a town where the Emancipator's image is everywhere, even on pocket pennies. To see him guarding the republic of print seemed right to me, since few other presidents have read (or re-read) with his intensity and care.

When the old Lincoln Library came down in 1974, the bust was saved, in poor condition. Bronze disease, said a restoration specialist at the Illinois State Museum. They dunked and scrubbed, brushed and waxed, reversing the ravages of exposure and corrosion, turning back the years. Today that bust dwells at the new Lincoln Library, same location, and once again Mr. Lincoln shows his wrinkles and rumples to advantage beside a window in the Sangamon Valley Collection, a major repository of Central Illinois history.

His sculptor was Frederick Moynihan (1843-1910), an Englishman who specialized in Civil War monuments. This 1904 piece captures a resolute Lincoln in his late years, wearing a wing collar, a soft bow tie, and a broadcloth vest and coat, with lapels made for tugging. On the acanthus-twined pedestal below is a one-word inscription, fitting his life and work: UNION.

William Howarth

Bust of Lincoln
Frederick Moynihan
Circa 1904

Sangamon Valley Room
Lincoln Library, the Public Library of Springfield
Springfield, Illinois

Abraham Lincoln never was a careful dresser. In this statue we see his wife Mary fixing his tie, straightening his lapels, and generally making him presentable for a public that wanted to see more of him. On the other hand, Mary did care about how she looked. She is wearing one of her famous shawls topped by the kind of fashionable bonnet no respectable Springfield woman would be without. Mary Lincoln has come downtown from the Lincoln home at Eighth and Jackson to do some shopping at Clark Smith's general store near the Pubic Square. Meanwhile the youngest Lincoln son, the irrepressible Tad, soon to be lifting a Confederate flag over the White House, is waving at his eldest brother. Robert is on his way to school and in life as in bronze, he is somewhat removed from his parents. As Lincoln suffers the sartorial fussing of his wife and looks out beyond her to national prominence, everyone is in character.

Jean H. Baker

Springfield's Lincoln
Larry Anderson
June 5, 2004

Old State Capitol Plaza
Sixth and Adams streets
Springfield, Illinois

"Why's he got his hand stuck out?" asked a little boy as his dad boosted him up toward the towering sculpture of Abraham Lincoln that graces Union Square Park in Springfield, Illinois. I hung around to listen to the father say Mr. Lincoln was waving at him. Not a bad guess. and the kid was delighted when he got up close enough to grab at Mr. Lincoln's oversized bronze hand.

Like most things involving Abraham Lincoln, there's a story that goes along with that sculpture. I often wonder what the thousands of tourists and scholars and school kids flocking to the museum across the street would think if they knew.

Here's the story.

I'm a fan of John McClarey, the artist who crafted the piece just prior to the opening of the museum in 2005. During his long career he has created numerous Lincoln poses for historic sites and collectors around the country. Some have gone to such unlikely destinations as Russia and Cuba. Yet I suspect this commission is the one he will never forget.

It began in McClarey's barn-like studio near Decatur, Illinois. State Historian Tom Schwartz and I had gone to see McClarey's larger-than-life clay rendition of Lincoln, just prior to its being shipped off to be cast in bronze. I will never forget walking into that barn and being surprised to see a nine-and-a-half-foot-tall figure of the President who saved the Union—digging a hole. There was Lincoln, formally dressed in a frock coat with top hat and gloves. He strained against the handle of an enormous shovel, one huge foot atop the blade. Finally, Tom broke the silence by asking, "Is this Lincoln the gardener?"

There had been, of course, a colossal miscommunication. The kind that can happen with a really big, really complicated library/museum/park project, when committees and government employees and designers and construction crews and artists are working simultaneously, but not necessarily in concert. McClarey's concept was literal—that Lincoln was the builder of a new nation, and building begins at ground level. But as the go-to guy for Lincoln, and a scholar in his own right, Tom Schwartz was absolutely certain that, pardon the pun, visitors would not dig this Lincoln.

I won't go into the drama that followed, except to say that John McClarey produced a new sculpture concept in record time, and he did it, I like to think, with malice toward none.

Ironically, he called it *A Greater Task*, borrowing from Lincoln's first inaugural address, but possibly because that's what we asked of him.

The sculpture has become a much loved, and much photographed iconic Lincoln, with the nation's most visited Presidential museum in the background.

The public does indeed dig it. I suspect Mr. Lincoln would too.

Julie Cellini

A Greater Task
John W. McClarey
August 11, 2006

Union Square Park
Springfield, Illinois

Abraham Lincoln loved stories. He used them to turn away wrath, encourage friends, disarm foes, and drive home legal and political points. Ever ready to hear one or to share one, Lincoln used stories to understand his world and to explain it to others, even us centuries later.

Sitting there, alone on a bench, he beckons the passersby to linger and learn from his story—history—and to share their own stories. His careworn face and weathered hands form their own sinewy narrative, silent witnesses to the joys, the tragedies, the failures, and the achievements of his life.

In one of those hands he holds a draft of his reflections on the most important story in his life—the conflict that has torn a great nation in two. Confronted with so great a conflict, Lincoln struggled to make sense of it. Finally, perhaps reluctantly, he concluded that God "has His own purposes." Still undaunted, Lincoln then attempted to give voice to the purposes, to give direction to the nation, to give all people a story we can understand and a mission we can fulfill. Even as we commemorate him, Lincoln inspires us to shape and tell our own stories. Abraham Lincoln loved stories.

Daniel W. Stowell

Lincoln on Park Bench
Mark Lundeen
August 11, 2006

Union Square Park
Springfield, Illinois

There it all is—or, better put, there he all is—the strength and the sorrow. The bust is a mighty thing, big and solid, like Lincoln in the fires of war, where he stood strong when other men would have quaked. This is not romance, or sentimentality: it is history, fact as real and stolid as the Borglum statue itself. But there is sorrow and sadness, too, around the eyes: outward and visible signs of his inward and spiritual anguish at the costs of the war and the fragility of union. I always think of Lincoln in these two lights, one of enormous courage and real power, another of uncertainty and a kind of fear—a fear of what God had chosen, as He must have chosen, to put America and Americans through, the bloodshed and the fires and the hate. Yet it was a fear he confronted more fully than nearly anyone else in the long history of the world. He stands with Churchill, in my view, as a statesman without whom everything—everything—would be different. This bust shows us anew that Lincoln was the most human of heroes, an American Henry V, who suffered as he led, absorbing the pain of his people and, in the end, on an April night, giving his life as a ransom for others. He was a man of strength whose death made a nation sorrowful. But without him there would have been no nation to mourn him.

Jon Meacham

Lincoln Bust
Gutzon Borglum
Cast 1930

Lincoln Tomb
Oak Ridge Cemetery
Springfield, Illinois

Thinking of the Second Time They Shoveled Up Mr. Lincoln

In September 1901, a quarter-century after thieves nearly made off with President Lincoln's body from Oak Ridge Cemetery, Springfield, Illinois, his casket was disinterred and reburied beneath tons of concrete.

1

The first time I thought of the second time
I blood-cold rushed, arm wrestling
wet logs and newspaper wads,
the morning's bevy of war and pestilence
banking my fire's oak, its reeking elm.
The woodstove purred, fat Tom Cat
asleep amidst slant sunlight,
shadows at half mast. Late April's
late snow cast death in the role
of fool poet's "sweet, sweet repose."

What's behind that door?

2

Then my shovel's smacking stone
beneath the lilies' conspiracy,
rock as pocked as the yearbook photo
I've claimed is misnamed –
Oh no, that's not me, baby!,
a notion the spirit Lincoln must've felt
when scheming thieves shoveled up his body.
Those ghoulish fools figured $200,000 an ample ransom
for The Great Emancipator's corpse, then nearly stole away
before cops arrived to clamp the irons. Clink, clink.

No wonder the government wondered,
"Is that Lincoln in there?"

3

It's my faucet's incessant dribble,
third time I thought of Lincoln's second,
and how, too, the Feds sent for plumbers
to solve their problem: "Misters Hopkins and Willey,
bring your tools. We've a job for you."
Potato soup bubbled on the stove, Monday's lost lunch,
then their bay mare's balky step, oil lamps and tall hats.
"Good sirs," Hopkins stuttered, awash in crypt light,
"you want me to open it?"

One minute the widow Smith's clogged drain,
the next a presidential coffin.

4

After that it's whiskey's work – conjuring
the kerchunk of plumber's chisel, kerchunk of lead,
dank kerchunk as the casket lid gave way.
"Now, look in there, Hopkins."
The plumber flinched above his cut six-inch square.
Below it, yellow mold stalagmites spritzed the broadcloth suit,
the starched shirt dust laden but spectral white.
The dead man's walnut knuckles had split seamed leather,
one final rebellion. (Lincoln so hated gloves
he drew them off when the Mrs. turned away.)

This, his tryst with eternity?

5

"What say you, Hopkins?" – this nation's question.
He nagged his nephew to fetch the whiskey.
Cork echoed, a swig, spooks feathered his lamp.
In that light, Hopkins cranked his face toward the man's
dusted with undertaker's chalk, powdered bronze,
their noses nearly touching.
In that light, he eyed what on earth becomes of us.
Then the beard. The beard.
In that sepulchral light, dead but not,
Hopkins uttered his line one first last time.

"It's him."

Kevin Stein

The Emancipator
Larkin Goldsmith Mead
October 15, 1874

Lincoln Tomb
Oak Ridge Cemetery
Springfield, Illinois

Two seated sentinels, different yet the same. A miniature bronze reproduction of the heroic proportioned marble original of the Daniel Chester French seated Lincoln quietly greets visitors to the Lincoln Tomb. Both the bronze in Springfield, Illinois, and the marble in Washington, D.C., are iconic representations of the Sixteenth President and serve as seated sentinels for the larger ideals and aspirations espoused by Americans.

The Lincoln Memorial has become a public confessional for Americans to present their petitions for change as well as express their thanks and gratitude. Marian Anderson, Martin Luther King, Jr., Vietnam War protesters, veterans, presidents, world leaders, tourists, and government workers, all raise their voices and present their petitions on the steps of this structure.

The Lincoln Tomb has also become a place for silent remembrance not only of Abraham Lincoln's life but the lives of countless Americans who served and shed their blood in the cause of Union and freedom. The longings of the inner spirit are too profound for words and receive their greatest expression in silent reflection.

Two seated sentinels, different yet the same. One watching over the national seat of governance while the other watches over the inner soul of American hope.

Jim Edgar

Abraham Lincoln Memorial Replica
Daniel Chester French
1922

Interior
Lincoln Tomb
Oak Ridge Cemetery
Springfield, Illinois

The Daniel Chester French bronze sculpture that stands in the Lincoln Tomb is very special to me because I own an original version of the same piece that is in the entry hall of my home. To me this statue shows the different parts of Lincoln. It shows a tall, serious man deep in thought. He is standing majestically, yet his head is bent with humility. Though his broad shoulders carry such a heavy burden, they remain strong enough to hold the challenge. The Lincoln revered by his country is also Lincoln the common man here. His hat is missing, taken off to honor those who gave their lives for this Nation.

There is debate as to whether this depiction is of Lincoln before he gave the Gettysburg Address or after he spoke those immortal words. If it was supposed to be the former, he is clearly deep in thought about his upcoming speech. If it is afterwards, he is overcome with sadness for all that has passed.

Would peace ever come for this man or for this Nation?

Shortly before his assassination, on Lincoln's last carriage ride with his wife Mary, they discussed traveling to California. They were making plans to finally enjoy their lives together. The war had taken a toll on him, and now, with that behind him, he could start a new life with Mary and their son Tad.

Lincoln did finally make it to California in the bronze image by Daniel Chester French that stands in my entry.

Louise Taper

Standing Lincoln
Daniel Chester French
1912

Interior
Lincoln Tomb
Oak Ridge Cemetery
Springfield, Illinois

The thirty-foot-tall, fiberglass Abe Lincoln, "the Rail Splitter," greets Illinois State fair-goers and tourists looking for "offbeat" attractions.

This statue suggests Lincoln's rail-splitting, flatboating, and pioneering past, which at first Lincoln was reluctant to use. Richard Oglesby, later thrice-elected governor of Illinois, thought Lincoln needed a "hook" to identify himself as an accomplished "man of popular origin." Recalling William Henry Harrison's successful "Log Cabin Campaign" of 1840, Oglesby enlisted the help of Lincoln's cousin, John Hanks, to recall some work that Lincoln had done when the Lincolns came to Decatur in 1830. Hanks identified some rails they had split nearby and samples were hidden until the Republican Nominating Convention met in Decatur in 1860.

When confronted with rails he had allegedly split, Lincoln cheerfully joked that he may not have split those exact rails, but he had split rails better than the rough hewn ones presented. The rail splitter phenomenon caught on instantly, and rails were prominently displayed in Chicago at the *Tribune* office and elsewhere. The National Convention embraced the symbol when Columbus Delano of Ohio seconded Lincoln's nomination by proclaiming that Lincoln "was the man who can split rails and maul Democrats." The Springfield Democratic newspaper countered that Lincoln was the Union-splitter, the hair-splitter, and the side-splitter (referring to the off-color jokes Lincoln supposedly told).

Mark A. Plummer

Abraham Lincoln the Rail Splitter
Carl W. Rinnus
June 1967

Illinois Building
Illinois State Fairgrounds
Springfield, Illinois

When I was a boy growing up in Sullivan, Moultrie County (in east-central Illinois, about seventy miles southeast of Springfield), I used to walk past the Lincoln memorial every day in the summer on my way to and from the park where we boys played baseball. It was a simple limestone plinth which said: "This marks the place where A. Lincoln spoke Sept. 20, 1858. Erected Sept. 20, 1912." When a new recreation center was built in the 1960s, the old plinth was moved to a new location several hundred feet to the north and west, and a new memorial was placed close by. It says: "This Memorial commemorates the speech given by Abraham Lincoln in Sullivan on September 20, 1858. The new memorial was unveiled by the Citizens of Moultrie County on September 21, 1968, during the Illinois Sesquicentennial Year."

Years later I learned that Mr. Lincoln had given his speech as part of his campaign for the United States Senate in 1858 against Stephen Douglas. Lincoln and Douglas both appeared in Sullivan that September day, but they spoke in different parts of town and at different times, so it was not a debate.

Douglas went first, starting a little after one p.m., speaking on the east side of the courthouse square. Lincoln was to talk later, at three p.m. at Freeland Grove, in the north part of town.

Douglas addressed a crowd of about 2,000 people, some sitting in seats around the stand, others standing in the courthouse yard or the street. My great-grandfather John R. Eden introduced Douglas, and my great-grandfather Martin was in the crowd.

The Lincoln supporters had brought a band to Sullivan to help attract supporters to their meeting. About 2:30, they formed a parade—without Lincoln, who had already gone to the Grove. The route of the parade took the 200-300 marchers past the west and south sides of the Square. The marchers then attempted to turn north but were stopped by the Douglas crowd. Douglas, who was nearing the end of his speech, remarked that he was used to that sort of "courtesy" in Northern Illinois, but had not expected it in Sullivan. He also urged the Democrats to allow the procession to pass. There was some angry shouting, and at least one brick was thrown, hitting one of the band boys. A little later, Lincoln made his speech of about two hours in the Grove, a stand having been erected under the elms for that purpose.

A couple of partisan newspapers tried to blow up the disturbance into a riot. But my grandfather I. J. Martin later wrote: "The affair was regretted by all sensible people, and no effort was made to exploit the event to the help or injury of either side. ... There was no riot and no fight."

The text of Lincoln's speech that day was not preserved. But it may not have been too different from what he said during the debate two days earlier in nearby Charleston. Those remarks may be found in the volume of Lincoln-Douglas debates which Lincoln personally saw through the press. *Political Debates Between Hon. Abraham Lincoln and Hon. Stephen A. Douglas,* Columbus, 1860. Newspaper accounts of the debates may be found in Collections of the Illinois State Historical Library, III, Lincoln Series, I, edited by Edwin E. Sparks, Springfield, 1908.

By crystallizing the issue of whether to permit expansion of slavery to the territories and by elevating Lincoln as the strongest spokesman in opposition to expansion, the Illinois debates helped make Lincoln president of the United States two years later.

R. Eden Martin

Lincoln Memorial
Fred Ben Watkins
September 21, 1968

Wyman Park
Sullivan, Illinois

Lincoln is smiling! Not an ear to ear grin, but enough to reveal his sense of humor that was well known to people around the Eighth Judicial Circuit. On his twice-a-year journey by horse and buggy over more than 400 miles of the "mud circuit," Lincoln freely shared his wit and wisdom in court and out. In county seats like Taylorville, which was the last stop on the circuit before returning to Springfield, the townspeople and the traveling band of lawyers and judge would crowd the boardinghouse to hear his jokes and stories. An event in Taylorville added to his humorous repertoire.

While Lincoln was arguing a case before a Christian County jury, a noisy ruckus erupted under the courthouse, which was raised up on eighteen-inch blocks. Some local pigs had decided that the area under the building was a perfect wallowing place. Concerned that the noise was distracting the jurors from his argument, Lincoln turned to Judge David Davis and requested him to issue a "writ of quietus" to silence and remove the noisy swine!

On the grounds where that event took place, Lincoln is looking down at the pig with the writ in its mouth, and we are smiling.

Ronald Spears

The Last Stop
John W. McClarey
May 28, 2005

Christian County Courthouse
Taylorville, Illinois

This giant, seventy-two-foot-tall fiberglass Lincoln statue arrived in Charleston, Illinois, the same year I did—1969. I was a sophomore in high school and to be perfectly honest, all the kids made fun of poor Abe. Everyone thought it looked like he was flipping the world "the bird." Poor Abe became a magnet for local ne'er-do-wells who scribbled graffiti over his enormous black shoes and lobbed rolls of toilet paper up under his coattails. Once, vandals even shot off the offending finger!

According to old newspaper reports, a group of enterprising businessmen commissioned the statue as a way both to honor Abe—after all, he debated Stephen Douglas here in 1858—and to bring flocks of tourists to town. Alas, the only flocks that came to town were the birds. Abe stood silent and forlorn at the edge of town until 1976 when he was loaded up on two trailers and carted off to nearby Ashmore to stand guard at the entrance to a campground.

Nearly forty years later, I find myself back in the area, gazing up at the gargantuan sixteenth president. Patched, re-painted, and sporting a re-attached finger, Abe looks a bit more dignified as he stands quietly amongst a grove of trees, holding court over a dozen chainsaw Lilliputian Lincolns depicting various phases of his life.

Diane Schaefer

Lincoln Colossus
Bob Eglett
1969

Lincoln Springs Resort
Ashmore, Illinois

A museum devoted to the historic Lincoln-Douglas Debates of 1858 is in Charleston, site of the 4th debate on September 18. Right outside the museum, the ground level, life-size sculpture of the debaters is very approachable. The two metal men appear as characters in one of those movies we've all seen where the action stops and just one character walks around and discusses his motionless colleagues. We can walk into this scene, peer over Lincoln's shoulder and touch his outstretched hand, or scooch down to Douglas's height and experience ourselves how Lincoln towered over the Little Giant. Unlike in other Debate sculptures, the two men face each other instead of their audience; they look directly into each other's eyes. They stand behind walls of solid rock; the space between them—the chasm—is sculptor McClarey's representation of Lincoln's "House Divided" metaphor.

Charleston is the site of some unfortunate words uttered by Lincoln, originally crafted to deflect Douglas's allegations of Lincoln's embrace of abolitionism. Lincoln claimed that he was "not in favor of bringing about in any way the social and political equality of the white and black races," a line that got applause from the mid-nineteenth-century audience. Twentieth-century activists with their own agenda have used the words at Charleston to accuse Lincoln of being a racist. They point out that Lincoln acknowledged that he did not favor allowing negroes to vote. These critics fail to recognize that in the seven years following the Charleston debate, the same man who spoke there would issue the Emancipation Proclamation, would announce a new birth of freedom in his remarks at Gettysburg, would shepherd through Congress a Constitutional amendment abolishing slavery, and would be shot dead by an assassin who just days before became enraged when Lincoln spoke of his support for the right of former slaves to vote.

Robert S. Willard

A House Divided
John W. McClarey
September 15, 2001

Lincoln-Douglas Debate Museum
Coles County Fairgrounds
Charleston, Illinois

"That government of the people, by the people, for the people." The ideas of what we call the Gettysburg Address appeared decades before November 1863. Lincoln himself put forth these notions too, but these specific words he used only two or three days before November 19, 1863, when he rode the train to Gettysburg. His genius shone. His words continue to be seen off and on. But by Lincoln's death, the Emancipation Proclamation became the American Gospel. The Gettysburg Address took its central place only slowly from the 1880s and 1890s. Neither did numerous Gettysburg monuments come to be completed until after the start of the twentieth century—nor did so many fully accept the genius of the speech. In 1903, Charles James Mulligan (1866-1916) created his vigorous orator in the Rosamond Cemetery, on a lovely hill near Pana. The words "Union soldiers and sailors" stood behind its white granite base, seven feet high, and in the front of it, Lincoln's thoughts are carved: "that we here highly resolve that these dead shall not have died in vain—that this nation, under God, shall have a new birth of freedom—and that government of the people, by the people, for the people, shall not perish from the earth."

Gabor Boritt

Lincoln the Orator
Charles James Mulligan
October 29, 1903

Rosamond Grove Cemetery
2 miles south of Illinois Route 16 on 2000 East Road
Rosamond, Illinois

I view every statue, every picture, every depiction of President Abraham Lincoln from the eyes of a descendant of slavery, from the perspective of a proud African American, a lawyer, but most importantly as a believer in the promise of America. Having been born in 1954, the year of the U.S. Supreme Court decision in *Brown v. Board of Education*, brought by Justice Thurgood Marshall, an Alpha Brother and fellow lawyer, I represent part of the promise of America, part of the continuing legacy of Lincoln and Marshall and part of the hope and vision of America. It is that promise that I see in the statue by John McClarey's Lincoln at Shelbyville. This statue in particular elicits feelings of hope and promise—admittedly in the dawn of his life; a time before the trials of war and the challenges of maintaining a less than perfect union. This statue represents a time of youth and vision, a time of hope and promise and a time of personal perspective before the horrors of war and the challenges of peace.

Jerry D. Blakemore

Let's Debate
John W. McClarey
January 2009

Shelby County Courthouse
Shelbyville, Illinois

"Ahh, it's good to be here with my friends—finally. That was a long trip. Do I hear music?"

Lincoln has just arrived on Courthouse Square and is stretching to get the kinks out of his back after traveling by train from Mattoon and by buggy from the Hillsboro station. He smiles, glad to be greeted by "Uncle Joe" Eccles, a good friend since his childhood days in Kentucky. Abe always enjoys these visits, catching up on the local news and swapping tales.

The satchel and umbrella recall that September day in 1858 when Lincoln appeared in Hillsboro as a candidate for the U.S. Senate. His opponent, Judge Stephen A. Douglas, had appeared at a rally in Hillsboro just a month earlier. The rain came in torrents on September 9, and Lincoln addressed an enthusiastic crowd of his supporters inside a circus tent at the Hillsboro fairgrounds.

Throughout his public life and even during troubling times, Lincoln sought out entertainment, theater, music to buoy his spirit. In Hillsboro, Lincoln faces the town plaza stage, the site for concerts, coronations, plays, pep rallies, and other community events. Abe smiles, knowing he is forever one with the audience—and among friends.

Nancy Bliss Slepicka

Among Friends
John W. McClarey
Maquette
To be dedicated on August 15, 2009

Hillsboro Plaza
Hillsboro, Illinois

Here the Lincoln of the Second Inaugural reaches out to the people. With the simplest gesture of his right hand, he seems to be imploring us to understand how "the war came" and what its bloody resolution means to our future. Meanwhile, from below, the symbolic figure of Columbia, representing the country he saved, reaches back toward Lincoln, as if to say, "Now he belongs to the ages." The pedestal declares that Lincoln died in 1865; the composition declares his immortality. In spring, with its garland of flowers blooming like a perennial wreath, this is a perfect arrangement of sculpture and situation. Yet in another sense, in its otherwise prosaic setting—for the statue sits in a modern traffic circle—the world goes on; cars and pedestrians come and go; the heirs to Lincoln's generation continue pursuing the American dream he did so much to preserve, perhaps without sufficiently acknowledging our debt to him.

Harold Holzer

Head of State
William Granville Hastings
September 7, 1904

Washington and Fayette streets
Bunker Hill, Illinois

This statue of young Lincoln before the Vandalia State House calls to my mind his remarkable boldness in denouncing slavery there when it was highly impolitic for an aspiring politician in Central Illinois to do so. On March 3, 1837, he and another member of the General Assembly, Dan Stone, filed a protest against anti-abolitionist resolutions that the legislature had adopted six weeks earlier by the lopsided vote of 77-6 in the House and 18-0 in the Senate. Lincoln wrote a protest and circulated it among his colleagues, all of whom refused to sign except for Stone, a native of Vermont who was not seeking re-election. Lincoln declared in the document, which he and Stone spread on the journal of the House of Representatives, "that the institution of slavery is founded on both injustice and bad policy," foreshadowing his great 1854 Peoria speech denouncing the "monstrous injustice of slavery."

Michael Burlingame

Sitting with Lincoln
John W. McClarey
February 10, 2001

Lincoln Park
Across from the Vandalia State House
Vandalia, Illinois

Abraham Lincoln and Stephen A. Douglas stand in Lincoln-Douglas Square near the Mississippi River, oblivious to the cold of a February morning. Lincoln, tall and gaunt, is in quiet contemplation; Douglas, short and rotund, is speaking. Observing these two protagonists, I am transported back to October 15, 1858, the day of the now historic Alton debate. Men are loading and unloading cargo from boats and trains; some passengers, both male and female, are boarding while others are disembarking. Still others are going to the train station nearby, where they will await a train, spend the night, or have a meal. Others are getting into carriages; still others are walking toward the city. Maybe some will join those listening to the debate. Vendors ply the crowd, hoping to sell their wares and to hear the debate. A few African Americans mill around the periphery of the crowd, listening to the candidates without drawing undue attention to themselves and their precarious position in this "free" state where slavery nonetheless exists. Many people bypass the debate scene altogether; they have more pressing business than to listen to two politicians pontificating, especially since the Illinois legislature, rather than the electorate, will select the U. S. Senator for the State of Illinois.

Shirley J. Portwood

The Last Lincoln-Douglas Debate
Jerry McKenna
October 15, 1995

Lincoln-Douglas Square
Broadway and Landmarks Boulevard
Alton, Illinois

This beautiful monument, unequaled by any other, was designed by sculptor Mrs. Nellie V. Walker, a member of the National Society of Daughters of the American Revolution. The monument, twenty-six feet long and ten feet high, displays Lincoln walking alongside a team of oxen drawing a Conestoga wagon. Lincoln is portrayed as wearing homespun clothing with a coonskin cap in one hand and stick in the other, a muffler encircles his neck and his feet are clad in leather boots. There are women and children walking beside the wagon, with two members of the family walking in front of the oxen. An angel's guiding spirit of destiny is represented leading them to a new home in Illinois.

This Abraham Lincoln monument located in Westport, Illinois, was commissioned during the Depression years. Illinois DAR members raised $15,000 by saving pennies for the project, and DAR member Mrs. William Butterworth donated $1,700 for the sculpture of Lincoln. The monument was presented as a gift to the State of Illinois on June 14, 1938, by the Illinois Organization of the National Society of Daughters of the American Revolution. In 1984, the retaining wall behind the monument collapsed. It took almost twenty years to get repairs made. I have always admired Lincoln for his tenacity, and I believe this monument illustrates it eloquently.

Inscribed on the stone face of the monument are the words:

In late winter of 1830, a few weeks after his twenty-first birthday, Abraham Lincoln passed this way with his father's family entering the state of Illinois for the first time.

B. Irene Black

Lincoln Entering Illinois
Nellie Verne Walker
June 14, 1938

Lincoln Memorial Bridge
Wabash River
Westport, Illinois

Lincoln the Lawyer, as opposed to his later, more political and bearded years, is the subject of this piece.

Most statues have pedestals for support, but pedestals often have the effect of elevating artwork beyond reach. The low, wide base here produces an open invitation to walk up and touch Lincoln. The effect is reciprocal—Lincoln's free hand is open, welcoming. It is no stretch to imagine thousands of photographs of children posed in a one-handed embrace by the Great Emancipator.

Lincoln's open hand, along with the soft kindness emanating from his eyes, balances the square-jawed certainty evident in this sculpture. Portrayed here one-third larger than in real life, he is all the more imposing a figure—imposing yet approachable, which certainly was the case when he practiced law in the old 8th Circuit of Illinois. The statue sits outside the actual courthouse in Mt. Vernon where Lincoln successfully argued for his client, the Illinois Central Railroad, in a tax case that was pivotal both to the state's economy and to Lincoln's trial attorney image.

In the April 1865 term of the Supreme Court of Illinois, Lincoln's death was memorialized by J. D. Caton, a former chief justice of the Court before whom Lincoln had appeared: "His hand was open to relieve the unfortunate, and his efforts were at the service of those in distress." The statue *Lincoln the Lawyer* extends that hand to generations to come.

Mark D. Hassakis

Lincoln the Lawyer
Alan Cottrill
September 18, 2008

Fifth Appellate Courthouse
14th and Main Streets
Mount Vernon, Illinois

The bronze bust of Abraham Lincoln located in Morris Library at Southern Illinois University represents for me the deep sadness of President Lincoln, the heavy burden that he bore, the physical and mental effects of the challenges that he faced, and yet, it also represents the ability of a willing nation to overcome even the gravest of adversities, to heal the deepest of life's wounds and to come together around common ideas, desires, and convictions. President Lincoln represented the best of unselfish leadership. Even in our darkest times, the hope that the same devotion to the great ideas of mercy, justice, and common purpose, which President Lincoln held sacred, will allow us to heal, to live, and to give ourselves to our fellow human beings in the quest for unity.

Glenn Poshard

Lincoln Bust
Gutzon Borglum
1930

Morris Library
Southern Illinois University
Carbondale, Illinois

The cold Jonesboro sky. A perfect backdrop for a clashing of the titans, or perhaps, a clashing of the "little giant" and the "well meaning baboon." The men stand poised in the black shadows that gently caress the white stone underfoot, a beautiful dichotomy as blatant as the heights of the two men. Are not the Lincoln-Douglas debates of 1858 a story of remarkable contrast between the established persona of the American politician and the emergence of a new breed of president, between the old virtues of an imperfect democracy and the hope for a true fulfillment of the Founding Fathers' vision, clashes as clear as the black and white in the photograph?

America shall forever be a nation of difference: differing beliefs, differing faiths, differing peoples. Yet it is how we as Americans embrace this contrast, how we interweave it into our national fabric, that shall truly test the fortitude of our character and the pureness of our hearts. A man who stood physically and ideologically at odds with the rest of his generation, a wondrous human anachronism, Abraham Lincoln envisioned a new nation, not plagued by its differences, but rather strengthened by them. Perhaps this is what the solemn man with a humble stovepipe hat sees as the sun sets over a black and white Jonesboro. Perhaps, but for now, both Abraham Lincoln and Stephen Douglas look with uncertainty upon a horizon destined to be ravaged by the incompatibility of their contrasting visions of America's future, just as the blackened trees juxtapose themselves against the white Jonesboro sky.

Lexi Wallace

Lincoln-Douglas Debate
Tom Allen
July 4, 2008

Lincoln Memorial Park
Jonesboro, Illinois

This bust shows a very kind and gentle Lincoln. He seems much younger than he does in later portraits. In January 1861 he has not yet undergone the trials of war. His brow is unfurrowed; his expression benign. His beard, still relatively new, is flattering. It softens a countenance that some observers had thought coarse, even ugly. The soft folds of his outer garment carry this effect further. Lincoln's pose, with head turned toward his right side, seems relaxed, yet dignified.

This Lincoln is paternal; it is easy to imagine that he might be looking at one of his children. He was an indulgent parent, and one can see it here. He has not yet undergone the grief he felt at the death of his son Willie.

Daniel Walker Howe

Lincoln the President
Thomas Dow Jones
January 1861

Private Collection
Chicago, Illinois

Worn by War, the bust sculpture of Abraham Lincoln by Thomas Dow Jones, is a brilliant image of a sorrowful yet prayerful President. You can see, sense, and feel the heavy weight of war on Lincoln's shoulders, a depiction of the deep pain on the soul of the nation that he was elected to lead. The sorrow inflicted on him, by the nation's brutal internal struggle for survival and the spiritual redemptive cleansing of the evilness of slavery, has clearly robbed him of his vibrancy. One has the feeling of seeing a powerful yet humble man whose destiny is to guide a selfish and bitterly divided nation toward the better angels of itself. It is the agonizing look of a parent hoping and praying that their rebellious child survives the often self-destructive battle of growing to maturity.

Most touching is the feeling that Jones has captured the essence of a reverent Lincoln. One can almost hear the conversation between Lincoln and God, as the words "well done my good and faithful servant" are being bestowed upon him.

Patricia James Davis and Robert J. Davis

Worn by War
Thomas Dow Jones
1864

Private Collection
Chicago, Illinois

This image strips away any indicia of economic, social, or political status and allows reflection on Lincoln—myth and man. As Illinois residents, we claim a part of his legacy. As members of the bar and partners in a firm once titled Stuart and Lincoln, we claim another part of his legacy.

Look at mixture of myth and man—from humble beginnings to rise to the Presidency; a career in law combining ability to define issues and communication of their resolution; delivery of some of the most eloquent speeches ever heard; and ability to maneuver through the quagmire of politics and bind a nation together.

Look at a common man—joking and telling stories; touched by family and friends; enjoying his boys and grieving at their loss.

Look at strength of character, resolve and wisdom. A product of his past, Lincoln did not dwell there. He lived in the present, dealing with challenges daily. Lincoln's true legacy lies in inspiration found in his gift to the future. His legacy transcends state or national boundaries, race, color or ethnicity, time or place.

Eleanor Roosevelt captured what I see:

The future belongs to those who believe in the beauty of their dreams.

Robert A. Stuart, Jr.

Lincoln
Martin Milmore
1865

Private Collection
Chicago, Illinois

He looks pensive, but determined. Fighting a war in this divided, young country costs human lives. But it is too important to allow justice and freedom to erode. "All Men Are Created Equal"—but to some, they are more equal than the others.

He is calm and confident. In extremely adverse situations, people follow leaders who have strong convictions, and who are able to maintain focus even with setbacks. Leaders are able to see beyond today and articulate what tomorrow brings. People put their lives on the line because they are fighting for their belief, and the future.

Guoxing Chai

With all the accomplishments Lincoln had achieved, he must have made mistakes. Lincoln was trying hard to avoid a repeat of past mistakes as he made the next big decision.

Aaron Chai

Lincoln From Life
Leonard Wells Volk
1866

Private Collection
Chicago, Illinois

He died only decades before someone could have recorded his voice and filmed him walking. Any student or lover of Lincoln always reaches the point where he wants him to move—up off the page, out of the painting, down from the pedestal. This bust by Gutzon Borglum, a model for what would be carved out of Mount Rushmore, moves a viewer with its peculiar plasticity: the slight cock of the head and the casual smile on the lips that seem just about to part—not in order to orate, but to continue conversing or maybe even tell an old New Salem story. Of all the stone and metal Lincolns, this one feels to be among the less guarded—a Lincoln that belongs not to the ages but to some ordinary moment; a Lincoln on the verge of re-animation. One almost expects to see an "on" switch near the figure's neck.

Thomas Mallon

Lincoln: Mount Rushmore
Gutzon Borglum
1905

Private Collection
Chicago, Illinois

Ron Schramm

Ron Schramm was born on the South Side of Chicago and now lives on the North Side. He is a graduate of Columbia College Chicago and served in Vietnam in 1974-1975.

Schramm is a professional photographer with an interest in history and architecture, both of which are the subjects of his photography. "With Chicago's mix of brawn and beauty and its unique location on an inland sea, I have an unequaled selection of unique world-class buildings. My photographs of Chicago and its architecture are taken in a studied way." By that Schramm means that he has spent most of his professional life looking for vantage points and from that point photographing Chicago architecture when optimum conditions occur. His search for vantage points keeps him busy year-round. He has conducted a seminar for architectural students attending the American Institute of Architects Forum in Chicago focusing on "vantage point."

Schramm's devotion to visual Chicago has produced images that have been used in his own book, advertising, television, architectural, product. As a commercial photographer, he has provided images for corporate clients, including CBS/Chicago, LaSalle Bank, United Airlines, University of Chicago, WBBM-TV, Opus North, Skidmore/Owings/Merrill and the City of Chicago.

He became interested in Abraham Lincoln and the Illinois statues while photographing county courthouses in Illinois.

He is a member of the American Society of Media Photographers, a past member of the Chicago Convention & Tourism Bureau, and an affiliate of the American Institute of Architects.

Schramm is married to the former Ann Buck and has two children, Zachary and Ellen.

Photographer's Notes

The images for this book were taken with black and white film using a black and white print as the basis for each page's record of a Lincoln statue. These images represent the most complete visual inventory of Lincoln statues in Illinois, both traditional and contemporary, that we were able to assemble. All of these black and white images have been made with Hasselblad equipment. In particular, the Hasselblad Supreme Wide camera has given me a view which includes visual information surrounding the statue that is as important as the statue because it places the statue in a very particular location. This camera yields a very sharp image on 120 size Black & White film.

Richard E. Hart

Richard E. Hart was born in Ottawa, Illinois, and was raised and educated in Springfield, Illinois. He attended the University of Illinois at Urbana-Champaign where he received his B.A. and his J.D. He was admitted to practice law in 1967 and has been a practicing attorney in Springfield for the last forty years. He is a partner in the firm of Hart, Southworth & Witsman.

Hart is currently President of the Abraham Lincoln Association and is a member of the Illinois Abraham Lincoln Bicentennial Commission. He is a past president and board member of the Sangamon County Historical Society, past president of Springfield Preservation, Ltd., a for-profit corporation that has restored and leased Lincoln-era houses in Springfield's German Settlers Row, past chairman of the advisory board of The Lincoln Legal Papers and past president and board member of the Elijah Iles House Foundation. In 1999, he was given the City of Springfield's Preservationist of the Year award. Mr. Hart suggested the format for the *Looking for Lincoln* project in Springfield and gave his personal research for use in this project.

Mr. Hart is the author of, "Springfield's African-Americans as a Part of the Lincoln Community," published in the *Journal of the Abraham Lincoln Association; Lincoln's Springfield: The Public Square (1823-1865); Springfield, Illinois' Nineteenth-Century Photographers (1845-1900)*; *Philemon Stout Cemetery, Ball Township, Sangamon County, Illinois; The Underground Railroad in Lincoln's Springfield; Lincoln's Springfield: Greek Revival Architecture on the Prairie; Lincoln's Springfield: The Early African American Population of Springfield, Illinois (1818-1861)*; and is the editor of *Early Sangamon County Antiques: The Barringer Exhibit.*

JEFF ADAMS
(1961-____)
Jeff Adams was born in 1961 and grew up in a small rural town in Illinois. In 1976 at the age of 15, he began working in a fine art foundry, Paragon Art Foundry, in Oregon, Illinois. During his four years at the foundry, he mastered all the technical and skilled craftsmanship involved in casting bronze sculpture and first sculpted and sold several original works. After receiving a degree in civil engineering in 1982 from Northern Arizona University, he returned to foundry work where his interest in sculpting was rekindled. In Arizona, he apprenticed with renowned figurative sculptor Clyde Ross Morgan. There he worked primarily in metal finishing and developed patina skills and techniques that were in demand throughout the Southwest. Since 1985, Adams has worked almost exclusively creating and casting his own sculptures. In 1993, he moved his sculpting studio and gallery to Illinois from Arizona. In 2000, Adams designed and built a bronze art casting facility, inBronze Foundry, in Mt. Morris, Illinois. He has reproduced and finished over 600 of his own sculptures. He has won numerous awards, exhibited in solo and juried shows, and has been awarded both private and public commissions. One of his best-known sculptures is *Paths of Conviction, Footsteps of Fate*, a bronze sculpture of Abraham Lincoln and the Sauk warrior Black Hawk.

TOM ALLEN
(1959-____)
Tom Allen was born in 1959. He now lives in Makanda, Illinois. He is the sculptor of Tecumseh at Glen O. Jones Lake in Equality, Illinois.

LARRY ANDERSON
(1940-_____)
Larry Anderson was born in 1940 in Tacoma, Washington. There he attended Lincoln High School where he edited the school newspaper. A statue of Abraham Lincoln by Alonzo Victor Lewis is one of the school's most notable landmarks. When his daughter was born on Lincoln's birthday, there were five other Lincoln High graduates in the waiting room with him. "Lincoln's been a part of my life for a long time," Anderson said.

Anderson holds a Master of Fine Arts degree from the Cranbrook Academy of Art and studied art at Lewis and Clark College as a protégé of Ivan Houser, the assistant sculptor for Mount Rushmore. Anderson has created over sixty-five bronze statues, and they are standing across the country. Anderson attempts to create very realistic, detailed, and historically accurate statues.

MAX BACHMANN
(1862-1921)
Max Bachmann was born in Brunswick, Germany, in 1862. He was active as an artist in New York City by 1899. He was a sculptor of allegorical figures including Indian heads. Among his many projects, he designed the allegorical figures of the continents for the Pulitzer Building in New York City. He died in New York City on January 13, 1921.

David Bentley
(1955-____)
David Bentley lives in Divernon, Illinois, but he was born and raised in Springfield. He served as a paratrooper with the Marine Rangers in Vietnam and in the National Guard 233rd Military Police Company. Including his military service, Bentley has been in law enforcement for 28 years. He has two children and three grandchildren and a wife who admits she watched with baffled amusement as he pursued his dream of creating a Lincoln worthy of the *Guinness Book of World Records.*

Phillip Bloomquist
(1935-2007)
Phillip Bloomquist was born in Wapello, Iowa. He died in Phoenix, Arizona.

Gutzon Borglum
(1867-1941)
(John) Gutzon de la Mothe Borglum, born on March 25, 1867, in St. Charles, Idaho, was an American artist and sculptor famous for creating the monumental presidents' heads at Mount Rushmore, South Dakota, as well as dozens of other public works of art.

At the age of seven, he moved to Nebraska and later graduated from Creighton Preparatory School. He was trained in Paris at the Académie Julian, where he came to know Auguste Rodin. In 1901, he returned to the United States and in New York City he sculpted about a hundred saints and apostles for the new Cathedral of Saint John the Divine. He won the Logan Medal of the Arts. A fascination with gigantic scale and themes of heroic nationalism suited his extroverted personality. His head of Abraham Lincoln, carved from a six-ton block of marble, was exhibited in Theodore Roosevelt's White House. and can now be found in the Capitol Rotunda in Washington, D. C. Believing that the "monuments we have built are not our own," he looked to create art that was "American, drawn from American sources, memorializing American achievement," according to a 1908 interview.

In 1908 Borglum won a competition for a statue of the Civil War General Philip Sheridan to be placed in Sheridan Circle in Washington, D. C. A second version was erected in Chicago in 1923. Borglum was active in the committee that organized the New York Armory Show of 1913, the birthplace of modernism in American art. But by the time the show was ready to open, Borglum resigned from the committee, feeling that the emphasis on avant-garde works had co-opted the original premise of the show and made traditional artists like himself look provincial. Later in his life, he settled in Stamford, Connecticut.

In his Mount Rushmore project, the initial pair of presidents, George Washington and Abraham Lincoln, were soon joined by Thomas Jefferson, and to make the theme of Manifest Destiny perfectly clear, Theodore Roosevelt. Borglum alternated exhausting on-site supervision with world tours, raising money, polishing his personal legend, sculpting a Thomas Paine memorial for Paris and a Woodrow Wilson one for Poland. In his absence, work at Mount Rushmore was overseen by his son, Lincoln. Borglum died in Chicago on March 6, 1941, and his son finished another season at Rushmore, but left the monument largely in the state of completion it had reached under his father's direction.

Giovanni Bucci
(1934-______)
Giovanni Bucci, one of Chicago's most renowned designers and artists, was born on May 23, 1934, in a small countryside village near Gorizia, Italy. As a young boy, he remembered Mussolini's Boy Scout youth gathering outside Biala during World War II. He came to the United States where his background in the electrical field opened the door for him to the television production line at Zenith Radio Corporation and later on to the Sun Electric Company automotive test equipment research laboratory.

His real passion was building automobiles. His first car was featured at the New York World's Fair Expo 54. His next car was without a metal chassis, a stunning, speedy set of wheels. Bucci toured Europe with it in the summer of 1967. His reputation spread and he was asked to design Indianapolis racecars, one of which was the World Champion Universal Oil, CAN-AM car.

During the 1976 Bicentennial he was hired to develop exhibits for the Italian Cultural Center. After this successful exhibit, he was asked to design and develop the permanent art gallery at the Italian Cultural Center with exhibits of Italians in Chicago. From these exhibits, he moved into trade show exhibits.

Gary Casteel
(_____-______)

Gary Casteel, a nationally recognized sculptor and painter, was born in the hills of West Virginia. He has always been fascinated with history and art. In the fourth grade, after seeing a picture of Michelangelo's David, Gary knew that sculpting was the profession he wished to follow. From the start, he recognized that raw talent was not enough to succeed. Casteel lived and worked in the United States and abroad, where he searched for professional sculptors in order to enhance his abilities by apprenticing under the masters.

Casteel's love of history and art are reflected in each individual work. Whether painting his beloved Shenandoah Valley landscapes, or sculpting a life-size figure, his artwork has always reflected a personal translation of the elements involved. After entering the national sculpting arena, Casteel found that his keen sense of history, talent, and drive for producing pieces in his personal dynamic style would thrust him into the demanding light of success with the Gen. James Longstreet equestrian erected in the Gettysburg National Military Park. Since then, Casteel's work has become highly regarded and requested by the National Park Service, state and local governments, corporations, and private enterprises.

In 2000, Casteel was honored by the National Civil War Memorial Commission with an invitation to design and sculpt a fitting memorial to honor those events and individuals, civilian and military, during the Civil War. The sculptor is currently working with a board of nationally recognized historians in determining the overall design content.

Alan Cottrill
(1952-____)
Alan Cottrill was born in Zanesville, Ohio, in 1952. After stints in college, the army, and truck driving, Cottrill founded the successful Four Star Pizza franchise and became an international entrepreneur. His business endeavors allowed him to travel the world on many U.S. government trade missions. Through these travels, Cottrill was able to visit the world's major art museums and galleries. In addition, he became an avid art collector and painted in his spare time.

In 1990 Cottrill touched clay for the first time and declared, "This is the mistress I've traveled the world in search of." He sold his business interests and dedicated himself full-time to becoming one of the finest figurative sculptors in the world. He moved to New York City and studied sculpture at the renowned Art Students League and the National Academy of Design. He also studied anatomy at Columbia Medical Center. He approaches his art with the same determination that led to his successes in business—sculpting seven days a week with a whirlwind energy that is unequalled. Intense, ambitious, and goal-driven, he has created hundreds of busts and figures, many at monumental scale. His works have been described as powerful, virile, and full of life, energy, and complexity.

Leonard Crunelle
(1872-1944)
Leonard Crunelle, a prize-winning American sculptor who specialized in figure and portrait busts, was born in Pas de Calais, France, the son of a coal miner. The family immigrated to Brazil, Indiana, in 1882 when Crunelle was ten years old. Then the family moved to Decatur and Pana, Illinois, where Crunelle worked in coal mines. In 1893, Leonard moved to Chicago, Illinois, to become a student of and apprentice to Lorado Taft, an art instructor at the Art Institute of Chicago. Under the tutelage of Taft, Crunelle established a reputation and career as a much respected sculptor in Chicago. He is best known for his pieces that depict American historical figures such as Abraham Lincoln, Sakajawea, and Richard Oglesby, a former governor of Illinois.

Jo Davidson
(1883-1952)
Jo Davidson was born in New York City on March 30, 1883. He attended Yale University before moving to Paris in 1907 to study sculpture at École Nationale Supérieure des Beaux-Arts. After returning to the United States, he was befriended by Gertrude Vanderbilt Whitney, who purchased some of his work. In 1911, Davidson secured his first solo gallery shows. In 1934 he won the National Academy of Design's Maynard Prize, and in 1947 the American Academy of Arts and Letters hosted a retrospective featuring nearly 200 of his works. He was one of 250 sculptors who exhibited in the 3rd Sculpture International held at the Philadelphia Museum of Art in the summer of 1949.

Although he specialized in realistic, intense portrait busts, Davidson did not require his subjects to formally pose for him; rather, he observed and spoke with them. He worked primarily with clay, while the final products were typically cast in terra-cotta, marble, or bronze.

Among Davidson's commissions are a design for a United States War Industries badge, a collection of pieces for the Government of France to commemorate the first victory of the Troupes de Marine, and bronze busts of the leaders of the Allies. His portraits of world leaders and celebrated personalities gained him international acclaim. He designed a statue of Henry D. Thoreau, the author of *Walden*. The statue is located at Walden Pond State Reservation in Concord, Massachusetts. In 2006, The Smithsonian Institution's National Portrait Gallery opened a permanent exhibition, *Jo Davidson: Biographer in Bronze*, showcasing fourteen Davidson works in terra-cotta and bronze, including portraits of Gertrude Stein and Lincoln Steffens. Davidson died on January 2, 1952.

Joseph Dux
(1857-1931)
Joseph Dux was born in 1857 in Philadelphia and came to Chicago in 1880, a graduate of Cooper Institute. Dux was an architectural sculptor, and the 19 markers erected by the DAR for the Lincoln Circuit Marker Association in the 1920s were produced by him. While the records of the association do not specifically identify the designer of the plaque, it appears quite likely that it was Dux. An 1894 record of his work is in the collection of the Library of the Art Institute of Chicago, entitled "Illustrations of Clay Models, Casts and Wood Carving Executed in the Establishment of Joseph Dux." The work shown there is of a similar nature to the marker plaque. It clearly demonstrates Dux to be capable of work of the quality done on the plaque. Dux died in 1931.

Bob Eglett
No information available; *fl.* 1969.

Avard Tennyson Fairbanks
(1897-1987)

Avard Tennyson Fairbanks was born in Provo, Utah, on March 2, 1897. His father, John B. Fairbanks, was an accomplished artist, having painted many of the murals in Latter-day Saints temples. At the age of twelve, he sculpted a clay rabbit and entered it into a contest at a state fair. The rabbit won first prize, but when the judge learned that a boy had sculpted the rabbit, he refused to award the prize. This experience made him all the more determined to become an artist.

Fairbanks followed his father to the Metropolitan Museum of Art in New York City. His work was recognized in a New York *Herald* article entitled "Young Michaelangelo of this modern day in knickerbockers working at the Metropolitan Museum." He spent time modeling animals at the Bronx Zoological Gardens. In 1910 and 1911, he received scholarships to study at the Art Students League. When he was fourteen, his sculpture was displayed in the National Academy of Design.

In 1913, Fairbanks went to Paris and studied at the École Nationale des Beaux-Arts, the École de la Grande Chaumiére, the Academy Colarossi, and the École Moderne. His works were exhibited at the Grand Salon. The outbreak of World War I led him to return home to Salt Lake City, where he continued his high school education.

Avard and his brother J. Leo were commissioned by the Church of Jesus Christ of Latter-day Saints to erect four sculpture friezes for the temple in Hawaii. Fairbanks did other religious, historical, and commemorative work throughout the northwest until in 1924 he entered Yale University, where he earned a Bachelor of Fine Arts degree. He then returned to Oregon to continue as a professor until he was awarded a fellowship by the Guggenheim Foundation. With this he went to Europe, where he created *La Primavera, Pioneer Mother Memorial,* and *Motherhood.*

After 1928, he taught at the Seattle Institute of Art. H then attened the University of Michigan, where he earned a Doctor of Philosophy degree in anatomy in 1936. In addition to numerous works for traditional settings, he designed the original radiator ornament for the Dodge Motor Company — a ram. He also created a winged mermaid for the Plymouth in 1930 and a griffin for the Hudson automobiles in 1933.

After World War II, he created three heroic statues to be placed in Statuary Hall in the Capitol Building in Washington D. C. He also began work on other monuments of Abraham Lincoln. He erected a heroic bronze in New Salem Village, Illinois, another at Lincoln Square in Chicago entitled *The Great Chicago Lincoln,* and another called *Lincoln the Friendly Neighbor* in Berwyn, Illinois. At Knox College in Galesburg, Illinois, he made bronze panels commemorating the Lincoln-Douglas debates. He placed four busts of Lincoln in the Ford's Theatre Museum—the youth, the rail splitter, the lawyer, and the president.

Of *Lincoln the Friendly Neighbor* he explained, "In the statue, Lincoln places his great hand upon the shoulder of youth as if on every young boy in our country, in every walk of life, and in every activity. Thus, symbolized in bronze, his guiding hand inspires every boy to greatness in the field he will choose for the future." Regarding the figure of the young lady looking up at Lincoln as she grasps his arm, the sculptor remarked, "There must be someone to guide our people in times of stress and dissension. Such is her expression of confidence in this great man. Her countenance represents the trust, the hope, and the admiration of America."

Paul Fjelde
(1892-1984)
Paul Fjelde was born in Minneapolis, Minnesota, on August 12, 1892, the son of a sculptor who emigrated from Norway in 1887. He studied at the Minneapolis School of Art, starting at the age of 15. He also studied at the Beaux-Arts Institute of Design and the Art Students League in New York, under Lorado Taft in Chicago, at the Royal Academy in Copenhagen, and at the École de la Grande Chaumiére in Paris.

Fjelde served as chairman of the Sculpture Department at the Carnegie Institute of Technology. He also taught at the Pratt Institute of Art in Brooklyn. He later was an instructor of sculpture at the National Academy School of Fine Arts in New York City. He was editor of the *National Sculpture Review* between 1951 and 1955.

When he was twenty-one, Fjelde sculpted a bronze bust of Abraham Lincoln for the people of North Dakota who wanted to celebrate Norway's 100th year of independence in 1914. Shortly afterwards, a copy of that original bust was dedicated in a park in Oslo, Norway. It is said to be the first Lincoln likeness installed outside of the United States. A third copy of the bust was installed at the Exchange Building at the Union Stockyards in Chicago on Lincoln's Birthday in 1916, and it remained in Chicago for the next fifty-five years.

Fjelde's sculptural works include the statue of Col. Hans C. Heg, leader of the 15th Wisconsin Regiment of Civil War fame in Madison, Wisconsin, the Wendell Willkie Memorial in the Indiana Statehouse, the bronze portrait of Orville Wright in the Hall of Fame colonnade, the John Scott Bradstreet tablet at the Minneapolis Institute of Art, and the Pioneers Memorial in Council Bluffs, Iowa.

Fjelde died on May 3, 1984, in Brewster, Massachusetts.

Fiberglass Animals, Shapes & Trademarks Corp., or simply FAST
Fiberglass Animals, Shapes & Trademarks Corp., or simply FAST, is a company located in Sparta, Wisconsin that designs and fabricates 3-dimensional objects. They made the Budweiser Clydesdales, the red-and-white-check overalled Big Boys, seen at corporate headquarters and at restaurants around the country, the 4-meter sunglass-wearing cow at the Holy Cow Casino in Las Vegas, and the 17-meter Jolly Green Giant in Blue Earth, Minnesota. You can see it in miniputts, water parks, and city parks all over North America. FAST has done work in more than 60 countries.

The artist emeritus of FAST is Jerry Vettrus, a legend in the industry. He started working with Creative Display, which virtually created the art form, before buying them out in 1983 and starting FAST. Soft-spoken and a true devotee of the craft, he proudly proclaims he has never taken an art class in his life. But his style is distinctive, realistic, and friendly. His masterwork is the mighty muskie at the Freshwater Fishing Hall of Fame in Hayward, Wisconsin. It took him nine months to sculpt this 145-foot-long fish in 1979, still the world's largest.

William Fothergill
(1930-____)
William Fothergill was born in Woodbury, New Jersey, in 1930. He studied at Sophia University, Tokyo, Japan, 1952-1953 and the Pratt Institute, Brooklyn, New York, 1954-1958. Fothergill was the recipient of a University of Illinois Faculty Summer Fellowship in 1963. He taught at the University of Illinois from 1960 to 1967. Fothergill's work has been in group exhibitions at the San Francisco Museum of Art, 1961; Ball State Teachers College, Muncie, Indiana, 1963, 1964; and Devorah Sherman Gallery, Chicago, 1966, 1967. His work is represented in private collections and in the public collection of the Illinois State Museum. The City of Champaign and the Champaign Park District commissioned Fothergill to do several sculptured pieces, including the Lincoln Memorial.

Daniel Chester French
(1850-1931)
Daniel Chester French, an American sculptor, was born in Exeter, New Hampshire, on April 20, 1850. His best-known work is the sculpture of a seated Abraham Lincoln at the Lincoln Memorial in Washington, D.C.

Reared in Cambridge and Concord, Massachusetts, he was embraced by members of the Transcendentalist community including Ralph Waldo Emerson. Author and fellow Concord resident Louisa May Alcott encouraged young French to pursue a career as an artist.

After a year at the Massachusetts Institute of Technology, French worked on his father's farm. While visiting relatives in Brooklyn, New York, he spent a month in the studio of John Quincy Adams Ward, then began to work on commissions. His well-known statue *The Minute Man* was unveiled April 19, 1875, on the centenary of the Battle of Lexington and Concord.

With the success of *The Minute Man* came opportunities to study abroad. After a year in Italy, French opened a studio in Washington, D.C. Additional trips to Europe and a friendship with fellow sculptor Augustus Saint-Gaudens resulted in more ambitious work, beginning with the impressive *General Lewis Cass* executed for the U.S. Capitol in 1888.

By the turn of the century, French was America's preeminent monumental sculptor. *The Angel of Death Staying the Hand of the Sculptor,* created for Boston's Forest Hills Cemetery; *John Harvard,* located at Harvard University; and a standing Abraham Lincoln at the west entrance to the Nebraska State Capitol are a few of the important monuments French produced during a long and productive career. In 1917, he designed the Pulitzer Prize gold medal presented to laureates. French died in Stockbridge, Massachusetts, on October 7, 1931, at age 81.

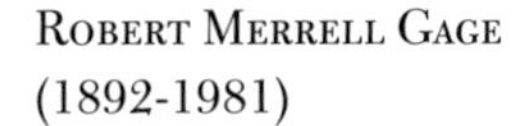

Robert Merrell Gage
(1892-1981)
Robert Merrell Gage, painter, sculptor, and lithographer, was born in Topeka, Kansas, on December 26, 1892. Gage was educated in the Topeka public schools and at Washburn College. After graduation he studied sculpture in New York City. He studied with Gutzon Borglum and Robert Henri, two exponents of the "American Theme" in art. Returning to Topeka in 1916, he set up shop in a barn behind his house and began his first public commission, the statue of Lincoln that stands on the Kansas State Capitol grounds. He was apprenticed to Borglum again during 1921-23 when he assisted in the designs for the Stone Mountain Georgia project. After serving in the medical corps in World War I, Gage taught sculpture at Washburn College and the Kansas City Art Institute. In 1924, he moved to Los Angeles for a position at the University of Southern California, a post he held until his retirement in 1958. Gage exhibited locally, fulfilled many sculpture commissions, and taught at Chouinard Art School from 1928 to 1930.

The winner of many awards and honors, he worked with stone, wood, metal, and clay as well as his format, which ranged from portraiture to architectural sculpture. His subjects consistently expressed major American themes. Deeply impressed by the writings of Walt Whitman and the example of Abraham Lincoln, Gage portrayed and interpreted the freedom and dignity of the American experience through the medium of his art. Some have called him "the American sculptor." Among his better-known works are his Pioneer Mother Memorial situated a short distance from his Lincoln statue at the Kansas State Capitol, his busts of Walt Whitman and John Brown at the Mulvane Art Museum, his Police Memorial and Veterans' Fountain in Kansas City, and his History of California frieze in Beverly Hills. Gage died in Laguna Beach, California, on October 30, 1981.

Jeff P. Garland
(1970-____)
Jeff P. Garland was born in 1970 in Springfield, Illinois. Jeff holds a BFA in sculpture, printmaking, and painting from Illinois State University and an MFA in Sculpture from Washington University in St. Louis. He is the former Chair of the Humanities and Fine Arts Division and Professor of Art at Springfield College and currently teaches at Illinois College in Jacksonville. Jeff is an established sculptor with numerous site-specific works across the United States.

Edna Goodenough
No information available; *fl.* 1970.

Rick Harney
(1954-____)

Rick Harney was born in Normal, Illinois, in 1954. He started his artistic career in 1975 working as an artist for a church interior designer in Peoria, Illinois. He moved to Normal in 1977 where he attended Illinois State University and received a Bachelor of Science in Art degree. While attending college, he continued to do church sculptures on a commission basis.

In the mid 1980s, Harney was accepted to Gilman/Gruen Gallery in Chicago and worked there as a woodcarver and woodcarving instructor for ten years. He has been featured in *Fine Woodworking and Wood* magazine and has won numerous national awards for unique, low-relief carvings.

Harney began to do public commissions in 2000 and has done a number of sculptures for Bloomington, Illinois—*The Lincoln Bench, Adlai Stevenson*, and *John Wesley Powell.* His works are in the collections of McDonald's Corp., Country Mutual Insurance, Illinois Wesleyan University, McLean County Historical Society, Central Illinois Regional Airport, and Asahikawa, Japan.

William Granville Hastings
(1868-1902)
William Granville Hastings was born in England in 1868. He studied art in London and Paris and came to the United States in 1891, where he was successful. He turned out a large amount of work including the *Soldiers and Sailors' Monument* at Pawtucket, Rhode Island, the *Soldiers and Sailors' Monument* at Orange, New Jersey, and the *Lincoln Monument* at Cincinnati.

In the center of the intersection in Bunker Hill, Illinois, stands his statue of Abraham Lincoln, a gift to the city by a Civil War commander as a token of appreciation to the Bunker Hill men who served in his company during the war. Hastings died in 1902 at age 34, before any of his statues were mounted.

Anna Vaughn Hyatt Huntington
(1876-1973)

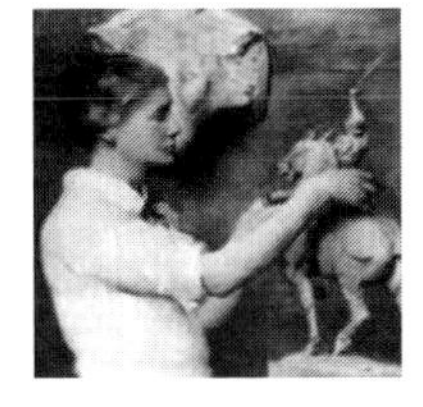

Anna Vaughn Hyatt Huntington was born in Cambridge, Massachusetts, on March 10, 1876. Her father, Alpheus Hyatt, was a professor of paleontology and zoology at Harvard University and MIT, and his influence was a contributing factor to her early interest in animals and animal anatomy. She studied sculpture in Boston with Henry Hudson Kittleson and at the Art Students League in New York City under Herman Atkins MacNeil and Gutzon Borglum. In addition to these formal studies, she spent many hours doing extensive study of animals in various zoos and circuses. Her earliest works consisted of domestic animals and dogs. She exhibited again at the Louisiana Purchase Exposition in 1904 and continued exhibiting throughout her life. She spent much time at the Bronx Zoo sketching and modeling the wild animals there. She won the Purple Rosette of the French Government and was made a Chevalier of the Legion d'Honneur for her equestrian group of Joan of Arc.

In 1923 she married the philanthropist Archer Huntington. In 1931 Mr. Huntington purchased 10,000 acres and built Brook Green Gardens near Charleston, South Carolina, as a home and studio for his wife. There she entertained and worked, becoming one of the most prolific American artists of the 20th century. She produced hundreds of models that were cast in bronze and some even in aluminum.

Because of her husband's enormous wealth and the shared interests of the couple, the Huntingtons were responsible for founding fourteen museums and four wildlife preserves.

Thomas Dow Jones
(1811-1881)

Thomas Dow Jones was born in 1811 in Oneida County, New York. He moved to Ohio in the 1830s and began working in Cincinnati as a stonecutter. He made his first portrait bust about 1841, and by 1844 had modeled a likeness of Henry Clay. Although Jones worked primarily in marble, he did produce some carvings in wood during these years. He also is said to have worked in bronze. Jones fulfilled several portrait bust commissions in the Detroit area in the late 1840s, and in 1850 moved east, working along the seaboard from Boston to Washington, D.C. In 1851, he settled in New York City, where he formed a partnership with S. H. Drennon. The firm produced replicas of portrait busts, medallions, and bas-relief portraits by Jones. It is possible that Jones traveled to London in the 1850s, as he produced several portraits of English subjects, including Queen Victoria. In 1861, the artist completed what would become his most popular work, a bust of Lincoln, for which Lincoln posed at Springfield, Illinois, in December 1860 and early 1861, just before leaving Springfield for Washington, D.C. and the presidency. Jones returned to Cincinnati about 1865 and continued to produce busts. He died in 1881 in Columbus, Ohio.

Andrew Jumonville
(____-____)

A resident of Bloomington, Illinois, Andrew Jumonville earned a bachelor's degree at Illinois State University. He earned a Master of Fine Arts degree at Virginia Commonwealth University (VCU). His commissioned artworks include installations for the State of Illinois, Danville Community College, Vermillion County Historical Society, the ESPN Zone (Chicago), and several private collections. He has taught college coursework at Illinois State University, Lincoln College, MacMurray College, VCU, and the Studio Art Center International in Florence, Italy.

Charles Keck

(1875-1951)

Charles Keck was an American sculptor, born in New York City on September 9, 1875. He studied in the National Academy of Design and Art Students League with Philip Martiny and was an assistant to Augustus Saint-Gaudens from 1893 to 1898. He also attended the American Academy in Rome. He is best known for his monuments and architectural sculpture.

In 1913 Keck designed a memorial plaque that was cast from metal that had been salvaged from the U.S.S. *Maine* after it had been raised in Havana harbor the previous year. Over a thousand of the plaques were cast and they are spread unevenly all over the United States. He died on April 23, 1951. According to legend, Lincoln attended a caucus of local farmers at the Seven Mile House (now Chicago's Senn Park) during his 1860 campaign for the presidency. To honor this legacy, the city donated *The Young Lincoln* statue by sculptor Charles Keck to Senn Park in 1997.

Keith Knoblock

(1941-____)

Keith Knoblock was born in Sandusky, Ohio, in 1941. He earned the BFA degree at Kent State University and the MFA at Ohio State University. He is proficient in filmmaking and has won awards regionally and nationally for sculpture and drawings. Knoblock has been a faculty member of the Illinois State University in Normal, Illinois, since 1967. During that time, he has enlarged both the space and the facilities for sculpture in the Center for Visual Arts. He developed an art foundry, enlarged welding facilities, and set up a studio for the fabrication of wood and plastic sculpture.

Knoblock's work has been shown in exhibitions at Western Illinois University at Macomb; Northern Illinois University in DeKalb; New York State University at Plattsburgh, New York; Hanover College in Hanover, Indiana; the University of Tennessee at Knoxville; Chadron State College in Nebraska; Illinois Wesleyan University; and Texas A & M University in Corpus Christi. His work also has been shown in regional juried exhibitions at Galesburg, Springfield, and Chicago in Illinois, as well as in Evansville, Indiana, and in several juried exhibitions at the national level.

Institutions which have made his work part of their collections include the Library of Congress, the Evansville Museum, and Western Illinois University, as well as the Illinois State Museum in Springfield, Lincoln Land Community College, and New York State University at Plattsburgh.

His wife, Doris, is a potter. Both Knoblocks have studios in their home in Normal, Illinois.

Marsha Lega
(1945-____)
I am an artist/sculptor and photographer. I am a wife, mother, and grandmother. I am an advocate for women's issues.

I am an artist working in metal, mainly stainless steel sculpture and furniture. I create stainless steel abstract contemporary wall and freestanding sculptures. I also work with weathering steel creating life-size and larger representational and architectural forms.

There was a time in my life that I questioned the name artist and photographer. Who am I to say that is my title? I no longer question my identity and I am at peace with my titles. Marsha Lega Studio, Inc. is located at 28 West Crowley Avenue, Joliet, Illinois.

Boris Lovet-Lorski
(1894-1973)
Sculptor and graphic artist Lovet-Lorski was born in Lithuania in 1894. He studied art at the Imperial Academy of Art in St. Petersburg where he worked briefly as an architect. In 1920, Lovet-Lorski moved to the United States and presented his first solo exhibition in Boston, just months after arriving in America. He worked for several years in Milwaukee, Wisconsin, before establishing a residence in New York City. He called New York home for the rest of his life, although he resided intermittently in Los Angeles from 1932 to 1934. In 1925, he became an American citizen. During his working life, he achieved prominence as a Modernist sculptor but in view of the fact that his work was mainly commissioned by private clients, his work began to slip into obscurity. Lovet-Lorski's sculpting career was cut short by crippling arthritis, which forced him to turn from direct carving to clay modeling for use in creating bronze castings. A decade after his death, a large selection of his major works of the 1920s and 1930s was discovered in his New York atelier, bringing his art into prominence once again.

Lovet-Lorski's style was eclectic but his work in the Modern style is the most individualistic and impressive. The female nude became his subject whether in marble or as a lithographic print. Alastair Duncan has written: "No other sculptor in America caught the prevailing French Art Deco mood as effectively or poignantly." Executing American commissions while living in Paris in the late 1920s and early 1930s, Lovet-Lorski established the standard for Art Deco sculpture created during the period in the U.S., with his highly stylized figures carved from exotic and often expensive materials.

Whether created from marble, granite, slate, onyx, stone, jade, lava, or metals, Boris Lovet-Lorski's sculptures are known for their technical virtuosity and their highly polished surfaces. His pieces were often romantic in style, with highly decorative qualities and a classic stylization of the human body that made them seem grander and "more real than real life." His torsos and female figures possess an abstract quality seldom seen in the sculpture of his time.

He was an associate member of the National Academy of Design and a member of the National Sculpture Society, as well as the Salons of Paris. His work is held in the collections of the Luxembourg Museum, Paris; Petit Palais, Paris; Bibliothèque Nationale, Paris; British Museum, London; Metropolitan Museum of Art, New York; San Diego Fine Arts Society; Los Angeles Museum of Art; Seattle Art Museum; San Francisco Museum of Fine Arts; Boston University; and Columbia University.

MARK LUNDEEN
(1958-_____)
Mark Lundeen is a native of Holdrege, Nebraska. He was educated at the University of Nebraska and received a Bachelor of Science degree in Business. Lundeen spent eight months in Europe studying the old masters. In 1981, he moved to Loveland, Colorado, and began a highly successful career as a sculptor.

Lundeen is a highly realistic sculptor with a fine sense of detail. His sculpture has fluid lines, balance, and integrity. He stages his artwork around the stories or emotions the characters portray which allows each viewer to find a different version. His work has a strong physical presence, whether it is an aggressive athlete, a pensive elder, or a shy child.

Lundeen was selected as the University of Nebraska Alumni of the Year in 1996. He has received the Philip Isenberg Award from the Allied Artists of America in New York City for his sculpture *Ragtime Cowboy Joe*, and *Westword* magazine of Denver awarded him Best Sculpture in a Public Place for *Mighty Casey*. He has also received Best of Show at the Best of Scottsdale Show in Scottsdale, Arizona, for his piece *Monkey Business*. He is a member of the Allied Artists of America and the National Sculpture Society.

Edgar D. Martin
(1865-1951)
Edgar D. Martin was principally an architect, engaged to design the Lincoln Circuit Markers. In 1906, Martin was later the third partner in the equally famous, pioneering Prairie School firm of Schmidt, Garden, and Martin. He left the firm and became State Supervising Architect of Illinois for several years, during which time he worked on the Eye and Ear Infirmary in Chicago. The Eye and Ear Infirmary building represented a unique commission that featured Prairie School design.

John W. McClarey
(1935-____)
John W. McClarey of Decatur, Illinois, specializes in the form and thought of Abraham Lincoln. He worked as a high school history teacher for 26 years. He has been sculpting for 25 years, with Lincoln as his most frequent subject. He has also sculpted such figures as Black Hawk, Robert E. Lee, and Ronald Reagan, and Americana, featuring such figures as an American farmer, a "country school marm," and a stump preacher.

His most prized commission was a bronze sculpture of Abraham Lincoln which was dedicated at the Russian State Library for Foreign Literature in Moscow in June 1998. At that same time, he served an appointment by the U.S. State Department to act as a "Lincoln Ambassador" to Russia. McClarey gave a number of talks about Lincoln and sculpture demonstrations. Other works of note include a number of prominent church figures who played an important part in the early history of Chicago and the Chicago Temple, and a commission by the United Methodist Publishing House in Nashville to sculpt the founders of Methodism for the 1784-1984 Bicentennial of American Methodism.

McClarey's other works include the *Abraham Lincoln Agricultural Award*, *Lincoln and Douglas* at Charleston, Illinois, and Lincoln at different periods for several Illinois cities and sites which include Vandalia, New Salem, Decatur, Peoria, Taylorville, Metamora, Hillsboro, and Springfield.

His heroic-size Lincoln for the centerpiece of the Abraham Lincoln Presidential Library and Museum complex was dedicated in the summer of 2006. In 2008, the sculptor completed work on a Lincoln bust for the Illinois State Supreme Court.

Other Lincoln works can be found in Havana, Cuba, and, Ashikaga, Japan. Many of his small Lincoln busts are given as gifts to foreign dignitaries and heads of state. The artist was the 2005 recipient of the Richard N. Current Award, the highest award given by the Lincoln Forum, and the first "visual historian" to receive this award.

The sculptor has a B.A. in Sociology from Millikin University, and an M.S. in U.S. History from Illinois State University. He is a frequent lecturer and presenter at schools, colleges, and other forums.

Jerry McKenna

(____-____)

Jerry McKenna was born in Connellsville, Pennsylvania. He has lived in Texas for over forty years. Nestled among the live oaks near the small Texas Hill Country community of Boerne stands a converted cattle barn, which houses his studio. He is proud of his Pennsylvania roots, but says, "I have traveled the world over and I have yet to find a more perfect place to work. It offers beauty, peace, and sunshine for most of the year." He has the distinction of holding both U.S. and Irish citizenship and he spends part of each year in Ireland.

McKenna began his formal study of art at the age of fourteen at the Gertrude Herbert School of Art in Augusta, Georgia. Later he continued his studies at the American Academy of Art in Chicago and at the San Antonio Art Institute. He received a Bachelor of Fine Arts degree from the University of Notre Dame, where he studied under Robert Leader and Dr. Stanley Sasha Sessler, and was influenced by the sculptor-in-residence, Ivan Mestrovic. He also received a Master of Arts from Webster University in 1981.

A former Air Force officer and decorated Vietnam veteran, his early recognition came from his bronze portraits of famous Air Force leaders. His work can be found in museums, parks,churches, public buildings, universities, halls of fame, and private collections around the world. In 1987, McKenna was chosen to create the Processional Cross for the mass celebrated by Pope John Paul II in San Antonio. He was named the 2003 Sports Sculptor of the Year by the All-American Football Foundation in recognition of his seventeen portrait busts in the Pro Hall of Fame, his sculpture of Knute Rockne at the College Football Hall of Fame, sculptures of Charles A. Comiskey at U. S. Cellular Field in Chicago, Frank Leahy and Moose Krause at Notre Dame Stadium, Elroy "Crazylegs" Hirsch for the University of Wisconsin, and many others. He is an Artist-Fellow of the American Society of Aviation Artists and a Member of the Coppini Academy of Fine Arts.

Hermon Atkins MacNeil
(1866-1947)
Hermon Atkins MacNeil was an American sculptor, born in Everett, Massachusetts, on February 27, 1866. He was a student at the Massachusetts Normal Art School in Boston. From 1886 to 1889, he was an instructor in industrial art at Cornell University and then studied with Henri M. Chapu and Alexandre Falguiere in Paris. Returning to the United States, he made two sculptures for the Electrical Building at the World's Columbian Exposition held in Chicago in 1893. In 1896 he won the Rinehart scholarship, passing four years (1896-1900) in Rome. He exhibited sculpture and won a silver medal at the Paris Exposition of 1900. He then returned to the United States and established a studio in New York City. He taught at the Pratt Institute, the Art Students League, and the National Academy of Design. His first important work was *The Moqui Runner,* which was followed by *A Primitive Chant*, and *The Sun Vow*, all figures of the North American Indian. *A Fountain of Liberty,* for the Louisiana Purchase Exposition, and other Indian themes came later; his *Agnese* and his *Beatrice*, two fine busts of women. One of his principal works is the sculpture in Columbus, Ohio, in honor of President William McKinley. In 1909, he won in competition a commission for a large soldiers' and sailors' monument in Albany, New York. He also made *Justice, the Guardian of Liberty* on the east pediment of the United States Supreme Court building. He designed the *Standing Liberty* quarter that was minted from 1916 to 1930. One of his last works was the *Pony Express* statue, dedicated in St. Joseph, Missouri, in 1940. MacNeil died in 1947.

Larkin Goldsmith Mead
(1835-1910)
Larkin Goldsmith Mead was born on January 3, 1835, at Chesterfield, New Hampshire. He was a pupil (1853-1855) of Henry Kirk Brown. During the early part of the American Civil War, he was at the front for six months, with the army of the Potomac, as an artist for *Harper's Weekly*. From 1862 to 1865, he was in Italy, being for part of the time attached to the United States consulate at Venice, while William Howells, his brother-in-law, was consul. He returned to America in 1865, but subsequently went back to Italy and lived at Florence. His first important work was a statue titled *Agriculture* to top the dome of the Vermont State House at Montpelier. This work proved so successful that he was soon after commissioned to sculpt a statue of Ethan Allen for the Vermont State House. Mead's work can be seen as neoclassical. His principal works are the monument to President Lincoln, Lincoln Tomb, Springfield, Illinois; *Ethan Allen* (1876), Statuary Hall, U. S. Capitol, Washington, D.C.; and heroic marble statue, *The Father of Waters*, New Orleans; the *Triumph of Ceres,* made for the World's Columbian Exposition, Chicago; and a large bust of Lincoln in the Hall of Inscriptions at the Vermont State House.

Martin Milmore
(1844-1883)
Martin Milmore was a noted American sculptor. He immigrated to Boston from Sligo, Ireland, at age seven, graduated from Boston Latin School in 1860, took art lessons at the Lowell Institute, and learned to carve in wood and stone from his older brother Joseph. He entered the studio of Thomas Ball of Charlestown in his early teens and stayed until the mid-1860s. His first sculptures seem to have been cabinet-size busts of Henry Wadsworth Longfellow (New Hampshire Historical Society, Concord) and Charles Sumner, both modeled from life about 1863.

By his 20th birthday Milmore received a commission for three giant figures (Ceres, Flora, and Pomona) for the front of the old Horticultural Hall, Boston, Massachusetts; they are now on display at the Elm Bank Horticulture Center. He subsequently designed the *Roxbury Soldiers' Monument* at Forest Hills Cemetery in Jamaica Plain (1867), the *American Sphinx* in Mount Auburn Cemetery (1872), the *Soldiers' and Sailors' Monument* for the Boston Common (1877), and a bust of Senator Charles Sumner now displayed in the United States Senate. After Milmore died at the age of 38, Daniel Chester French created a very fine memorial tribute entitled *Death and the Sculptor* for Milmore's grave in Forest Hills Cemetery, Jamaica Plain, Massachusetts.

Marshall Mitchell
(1917-2001)
Marshall Mitchell was born on January 29, 1917, in Springfield, Illinois. His artistic talent was recognized by his teachers during his early school years. By the time he attended high school, he had sold a professional illustration and had attended a summer session at the Art Institute of Chicago. In 1974, Mitchell sold his commercial art business, the largest in the Midwest, and moved to a farm west of Springfield. There he focused on sculpture and created his first bronze, developing a national reputation as a western sculptor.

Frederick Moynihan
(1843-1910)
Frederick Moynihan was an American sculptor, born on the Isle of Guernsey in 1843. Moynihan studied at the Royal Academy in London before immigrating to the United States. He is best remembered for creating monuments commemorating the American Civil War, including *Pennsylvania's Ninth "Lochiel" Veteran Cavalry Monument*, Chickamauga and Chattanooga National Military Park, Fort Oglethorpe, Georgia 1894; *Georgia State Monument,* Chickamauga and Chattanooga National Military Park, Fort Oglethorpe, Georgia 1899; *Griffin A. Stedman Monument*, Hartford, Connecticut, 1900; *General Gustavus Sniper*, equestrian, Syracuse, New York, 1904; and *J.E.B. Stuart*, equestrian, Richmond, Virginia, 1907. He died in New York City on January 9, 1910.

Don Morris

(1936-____)

Don Morris, sculptor and woodcarver, was born near Xenia, Illinois, in 1936 and graduated from Flora High School. He served in the Air Force as a medic and a hospital technician. After his service, he later moved to Rock Falls, Illinois, where he worked in a steel plant and built houses. He developed his skills as a carver in his retirement years and soon began teaching woodcarving and sculpture. His first major commission was a bronze statue of George Rogers Clark that stands in a park in Flora, Illinois.

Charles James Mulligan

(1866-1916)

Charles James Mulligan was a Chicago-based American sculptor, born in 1866. He worked as a student in the Paris studio of Auguste Rodin. He located in Chicago, Illinois, and in 1895 was an evening student at the Art Institute of Chicago where he had a studio through the 1920s. There he and fellow students formed The Palette & Chisel Academy of Fine Arts to foster growth in the visual arts, provide a place for serious artists to work, and enrich the community with programs of art education, appreciation, and exhibitions. He was able to persuade Lorado Taft to rent the fledgling organization part of his seventh-floor studio in the old Athenaeum Building on Van Buren Street in Chicago.

Andrew O'Connor, Jr.

(1874-1941)

Andrew O'Connor, Jr., was a quiet, brilliant American sculptor of monuments and portrait busts. He was born in Worcester, Massachusetts, the son of a sculptor of Irish descent of the same name. He studied under his father and probably worked for the sculptor William Ordway Partridge preparing work for the Chicago World's Fair in 1891-92. In London from 1894 to 1898, he met John Singer Sargent and assisted him on reliefs for the Boston Library decorations. On his return to America, he was commissioned through the sculptor Daniel Chester French to make bronze doors for St Bartholomew's Church in New York. From 1903 to 1914, he lived in Paris, where his work was influenced to some extent by Dalou and Rodin, then from 1914 to the mid 1920s at Paxton, Massachusetts. In 1906, his first one-man exhibition was at the Kunstsalon Walther Zimmermann in Munich. He received various commissions for funerary and public monuments, including the monument to Abraham Lincoln at Springfield, Illinois, an equestrian statue of Lafayette at Baltimore, and the Theodore Roosevelt memorial at Glenview, near Chicago.

O'Connor spent his last years in Europe, first in Paris, and then from about 1932 in Ireland and in London. He died in Dublin in 1941.

Abbott Lawrence Pattison
(1916-1999)
Abbott Lawrence Pattison was born in Chicago in 1916, one of seven children. Pattison attended Yale University, graduating with a Bachelor of Arts degree and a Bachelor of Fine Arts degree. He began his professional career as a creator and teacher of art, which was interrupted in 1942 when he joined the Navy. Stationed in the Pacific, he commanded a ship of 125 men. After the war he resumed his career as a sculptor. He, his wife Mary, and their four children lived in Winnetka, Illinois, for 35 years until 1993 when he moved to Maine.

Pattison taught at The Art Institute of Chicago, the North Shore Art League, and the Skowhegan School of Art in Maine. He was sculptor in residence at the University of Georgia, held numerous one-man exhibitions, and was honored with prestigious awards and prizes. More than 20 of Pattison's works are located in and around the Chicago area, including a bas-relief on the front wall of the house at 660 Pine Street in Winnetka, and sculptures at New Trier East High School, St. Mary's Church in Lake Forest, the Northbrook and Glenview Public Libraries, and the campus of Chicago State University. His sculptures are included in the permanent collections of the Art Institute of Chicago and the rotunda of the Illinois State Capitol.

Carl W. Rinnus
(1912-1993)
Carl W. Rinnus was a German immigrant who helped pay his family's bills by delivering Western Union telegrams. At age 16, he went to work in the kitchen of the old Leland Hotel in Springfield, Illinois. As an adult, Rinnus resided in Athens, Illinois, and worked in Springfield as a window decorator at both Herndon's and Bressmer's department stores, known for sophisticated and colorful displays. He was approached by Illinois State Fair officials to create a giant figure of the ax-wielding Lincoln of the New Salem years. The thirty-foot figure, *The Railsplitter,* was erected in late June of 1967, about six weeks before the opening of that year's state fair. It was constructed of fiberglass and was assembled around a wire-screen frame. Lincoln's legs were fabricated around two telephone poles. Garishly colored like other roadside giants of that day, the young Lincoln holds his ax as if he was just taking a break from work.

Augustus Saint-Gaudens
(1848-1907)
Augustus Saint-Gaudens, born in Dublin, Ireland, on March 1, 1848, was the American sculptor of the Beaux-Arts generation who most embodied the ideals of the "American Renaissance." Raised in New York, after his parents immigrated to America when he was six months of age, he was apprenticed to a cameo-cutter, but also took art classes at the Cooper Union and the National Academy of Design. At 19, his apprenticeship completed, he traveled to Paris where he studied in the atelier of François Jouffroy at the École des Beaux-Arts. In 1870, he left Paris for Rome, to study art and architecture, and worked on his first commissions. There he met an American art student, Augusta Homer, whom he married in 1877. In New York he was a member of the Tilers, a group of prominent artists and writers, including Winslow Homer, William Merritt Chase, and Arthur Quartley.

In 1876 he received his first major commission, a monument to Civil War Admiral David Farragut, in New York's Madison Square. His friend Stanford White designed an architectural setting for it, and when it was unveiled in 1881, its naturalism, its lack of bombast, and its siting combined to make it a tremendous success, and Saint-Gaudens's reputation was established.

The commissions followed fast: the colossal *Standing Lincoln* in Lincoln Park, Chicago in a setting by architect Stanford White, 1884-1887, considered the finest portrait statue in the United States; and a long series of funerary monuments and busts: the *Adams Memorial*, the *Peter Cooper Monument,* and the *John A. Logan Monument.* The greatest of these is the bronze bas-relief that forms the *Robert Gould Shaw Memorial* on Boston Common, 1884-1897, commemorating Shaw and the African-American 54th Massachusetts Volunteer Infantry. Saint-Gaudens labored on it for fourteen years, and even after the public version had been unveiled, he continued with further versions.

Saint-Gaudens also maintained an interest in numismatics. He designed the twenty-dollar "double eagle" gold piece for the U.S. Mint in 1905-7, still considered the most beautiful American coin ever issued, as well as the $10 "Indian Head" gold eagle, both of which were minted from 1907 until 1933. In his later years he founded the "Cornish Colony," an artistic colony that included notable painters, sculptors, writers, and architects at Cornish, New Hampshire.

His prominence brought him students, and he was an able and sensitive teacher. He tutored young artists privately, taught at the Art Students League, and took on a large number of assistants. He was an artistic advisor to the World's Columbian Exposition of 1893, an avid supporter of the American Academy in Rome, and part of the MacMillan Commission, which brought into being L'Enfant's long-ignored master-plan for the nation's capital. Throughout his career he made a specialty of intimate private portrait panels in sensitive, very low relief, which owed something to the Florentine Renaissance.

Diagnosed with cancer in 1900, he decided to live in Cornish at his Federal house with barn-studio set in the handsome gardens he had made, where he and his family had been spending summers since 1885—though not in retirement. Despite diminishing energy, he continued to work, producing a steady stream of reliefs and public sculpture. In 1904, he was one of the first seven chosen for membership in the American Academy of Arts and Letters. That same year the large studio burned, with the irreplaceable loss of the sculptor's correspondence, his sketch books, and many works in progress. He died on August 3, 1907, at Cornish, New Hampshire.

Lorado Taft
(1860-1936)
Lorado Zadoc Taft was an American sculptor, writer, and educator, born in Elmwood, Illinois, on April 29, 1860. After being homeschooled by his parents, Taft earned his bachelor's degree (1879) and master's degree (1880) from the University of Illinois where his father, Don Carlos Taft, was professor of geology. Lorado Taft studied art informally with a faculty friend of the family. In 1880, he left for Paris to study sculpture. In Paris he attended the École des Beaux-Arts where he studied with Augustin Dumont, Jean Marie Bienaimé (Bonnassieux), and Jules Thomas.

Upon returning to Chicago in 1886, he set up a studio as a sculptor and began teaching at the Art Institute of Chicago, a post he retained until 1929. He married Carrie Bartlett of Boston, but she died in childbirth the following year. Taft's sculptural work, including commissions for the 1893 World's Fair in Chicago, gained him fame as an artist. In 1896 he married a cousin of his first wife, Ada Bartlett. In 1903, Taft published *History of American Sculpture*, the country's first serious history of American plastic arts and a work that Taft is better known for (except perhaps in Chicago) than his many sculptures. His revised version, published in 1925, was to remain the standard reference on the subject until Wayne Craven published *Sculpture in America* in 1968.

Taft's book followed a vigorous lecture circuit and courses at the new University of Chicago. He also moved his studio to the Midway, across from the University of Chicago. In 1909 he was elected to the National Academy of Design. From 1925 to 1929, he was a member of the National Fine Arts Commission.

Taft referred to himself as an "art missionary." He strove in his books, both on the history of art and art appreciation, to make the American public "less casual" about their arts. Taft's sculpture was conservative, in a beaux-arts tradition.

In 1892, when Chicago was preparing for the World's Columbian Exposition of 1893, head architect Daniel Burnham expressed concern to Taft that the sculptural adornments to the buildings might not be finished on time. Taft asked if he could employ some of his female students as assistants (women as sculptors were not an accepted reality at that time) for the Horticultural Building. Burnham responded with the classic reply, "hire anyone, even white rabbits if they'll do the work." From that arose a group of talented women sculptors who were to retain the name "the White Rabbits." In general, history has given Taft credit for helping to advance the status of women as sculptors.

As he grew older his eloquent speaking skills and compelling writing led Taft, along with Frederick Ruckstull, to the forefront of sculpture's conservative ranks, where he often served as a spokesperson against the modern and abstract tendencies that developed in sculpture during his lifetime. Taft's frequent lecture tours for the Chautauqua also gave him a certain measure of celebrity.

In 1921 Taft published *Modern Tendencies in Sculpture*, a compilation of his Scammon Lectures at the Art Institute of Chicago. The book continues to be not only an excellent survey of American sculpture in the early years of the 20th century but still provides one of the best overviews (in English) of the European sculpture scene at that time.

Taft suffered a paralytic stroke and died in Chicago on October 30, 1936, following a subsequent heart attack.

Carl Tolpo
(1901-1975)
Carl Tolpo and his artist wife, Lily, settled in northwestern Illinois. His career as painter/sculptor included numerous official and public pieces, including those listed in the Smithsonian National Portrait Gallery Catalog of American Portraits. For over 15 years with their three children, Ti, Carolyn, and Vincent, they summered in Yellowstone Park. Reproductions of his Yellowstone and Grand Canyon paintings have been sold since 1939. In one survey, his heroic head sculpture of Abraham Lincoln enjoys ranking among the five best works on Lincoln.

Lily Tolpo
(1917-____)
Lily Tolpo was born in Chicago, Illinois, in 1917. Her nickname was "The Little Artist" in her preschool years as she exhibited artistic skill at an early age. She attended Chicago public schools where she carved a sculpture in soap that was exhibited in the Smithsonian Museum in Washington. She learned to play the violin at an early age and music provided inspiration for her art. She attended the Chicago Academy of Fine Arts in 1935 and made her professional debut in 1941 in a one-artist show at the Chicago Drake Hotel. She married Carl Tolpo in 1941, and the two of them formed a husband and wife artist team. Lily has worked from Illinois studios for over six decades, creating art that includes paintings as well as sculptures. On April 12, 2006, the Illinois House of Representatives passed a resolution recognizing Lily for her artistic talent and dedication to artwork and her community. Her works grace extensive private and public sites, including: *The Lincoln and Douglas in Debate* statue, in Freeport, Illinois, *The Law and Justice Chandelier* of the County Court Building in Waukegan, Illinois; *Whoffle Koenig The Magic Dragon*, in Krape Park, *Commissioner's Garden*, Freeport, Illinois; and *Julia Dent Grant,* First Lady Park, in Galena, Illinois.

Fred M. Torrey

(1884-1967)

Fred M. Torrey, an American sculptor, was born in Fairmont, West Virginia, on July 29, 1884. He graduated from high school and worked as a window decorator until 1909 when he enrolled in the Art Institute of Chicago. For a number of years he was an associate of Lorado Taft. After he married Mabel Landrum in 1916, the couple joined the Midway Studios Colony in Chicago, a cooperative group of sculptors. In 1948, the couple purchased a studio in Chicago where they lived and worked until 1957.

Albert Louis Van den Berghen

(1850-1921)

Albert Louis Van den Berghen was born in Vilvorde, Belgium, on September 8, 1850. After studying sculpture in Brussels, he came to the United States in 1876 and continued his studies in New York and Chicago. The statue of Abraham Lincoln in Clinton that was dedicated in 1931 is a replica of the original bronze work that Van den Bergen sculpted for the city of Racine, Wisconsin.

Anthony Vestuto

(1929-____)

Anthony Vestuto was born on May 27, 1929, in Chicago, Illinois, and attended schools there. He served as an aerial and ground photographer in the U. S. Air Force from 1948-1952.

Vestuto obtained his Bachelor of Fine Arts in painting at Illinois Wesleyan University and Masters of Fine Arts in sculpture and painting at Southern Illinois University. During his academic years, he had teaching assistantships and then served on the faculty at both universities following the completion of his degrees.

Vestuto's teaching experience also includes many workshops and short courses at Indiana University, University of Illinois, Lincoln at College-Bloomington-Normal, and Heron School of Art at Indianapolis. He was employed at Hadley-Luzerne Central School at Lake Luzerne, New York (1957-1960) and Brown County School Corp., Nashville, Indiana (1974-1992) as a teacher.

Vestuto has created commissioned sculptures for permanent displays in Decatur and Springfield, Illinois. In the eastern and Midwestern areas of the U. S., his work has been exhibited in one-man and juried art shows.

Vestuto met and married Patricia Payne Vestuto while both were art students at Illinois Wesleyan. They owned and operated Brettony Fine Arts and Crafts Center, in Bloomington, Indiana, in the 1960s. After retiring from teaching in 1992, Vestuto continues to work, travel, and consult with individual artists in Florida, California, Indiana, Illinois, and Arizona.

In his travels, Vestuto has been drawn to the decaying and abandoned barns in the rural areas. "The texture, the geometric lines give each barn a different personality."

Jerry Vettrus
See entry for Fiberglass Animals, Shapes & Trademarks Corp.

Leonard Wells Volk
(1828-1895)

Leonard Wells Volk was an American sculptor, born on November 7, 1828, at Wellstown (now Wells), Hamilton County, New York. He first followed the trade of a marble cutter with his father at Pittsfield, Massachusetts. In 1848 he opened a studio at St Louis, Missouri, and in 1855 was sent by his wife's cousin, politician Stephen A. Douglas, to Rome to study. Returning to America in 1857, he settled in Chicago, where he helped to establish an Academy of Design and was for eight years its head. Among his principal works: the Douglas monument at Chicago, Illinois, the Soldiers' and Sailors' Monument at Rochester, New York, statues of Abraham Lincoln and Stephen A. Douglas in the Illinois State Capitol at Springfield, Illinois, a statue of General James Shields in Statuary Hall, United States Capitol, and statues of Elihu B.Washburne, Zachariah Chandler, and David Davis. In 1860 he made a life mask of Lincoln, which has been very frequently reproduced. He died on August 19, 1895.

Fran Volz
(1958-____)
Fran Volz was born the 5th of 10 children in Menasha, Wisconsin. At the age of 9 his family moved to Mississippi. Having an unusual name and new surroundings added to his already shy nature. Volz learned, however, that he could amuse his classmates and make friends by drawing cartoons. By high school, he earned a recognition award in one of his drawing courses.

As a young man, Volz regularly spent hours with his father in their home workshop fixing and fabricating things. For safety reasons, Volz was not allowed to use the power tools, which only served to make him more proficient with many of the hand tools he uses today.

Volz earned a bachelor's degree in Religious Studies from St. Norbert College in Wisconsin. Many of his creations are influenced by his religious upbringing and background. Volz also served in the United States Air Force. He began his sculpting career on a cold winter's day in 1987. Looking to build a snowman, he decided to shape it into a cartoon Smurf instead. Encouraged by passing motorists, he realized he had created something special. Since that time, Volz has been recognized for his snow creations and has won state snow-sculpting competitions. Because of his elaborate snow sculptures, Volz is featured in newspapers at least a dozen times yearly. He is also visited by local TV and radio personalities who feature his works on their programs. He put together an hour instructional video that regularly airs on a local public access station during the winter months. In 2004 he organized the Chicago Snow Competition.

While Volz enjoys working with snow, his real love is creating monumental statues in bronze. He likes the permanence of bronze and the classical appearance these works have. Volz has been influenced by a variety of sources. He enjoys the classical styles of such artists as Michelangelo, DaVinci, Rodin, and Houdon; the whimsical subjects of Norman Rockwell; the dynamic poses of Marvel Comics superheroes, and the fluid, flowing lines of Disney and Vargas characters. As with his snow sculptures, Volz likes to create bronze works that touch people. For this reason, he concentrates on human form compositions. Volz is essentially a self-taught sculptor, learning mainly from observing, studying, researching, and experimenting. He did receive some formal training in the bronzing process by working for a short time as an apprentice to a local bronze sculptor. Most of Volz's time these days is spent working on commissioned pieces of loved ones or monuments to honor historical heroes or events.

Nellie Verne Walker
(1874 -1973)
Nellie Verne Walker was an American sculptor, born on December 8, 1874, in Red Oak, Iowa. She was the daughter of Jane Lindsay Walker and Everett Walker, a stonecarver and monument maker. By the age of 17 she was allowed to use her father's tools and began making her own sculpture. Her first noteworthy work was a bust of Abraham Lincoln that was displayed at the World's Columbian Exposition in 1893. She was to return to the theme of Lincoln again in her career.

Unable to afford to go to art school, Walker worked as a legal secretary for six years before she could obtain enough money to attend the Art Institute of Chicago. At 4' 8" and less than 100 pounds she seemed an unlikely candidate to be able to succeed at the very physical demands placed on a sculptor, but the teacher, Lorado Taft, decided to give her a chance and they were to remain friends and co-workers for the rest of their lives. It is likely that her years as a secretary explain why Taft chose to hire her as his secretary, but it was not long before Walker had moved up to lecturing and doing demonstrations at the Art Institute. Not long thereafter she began getting her own commissions and so moved into studio space in the famous (in sculpture circles) Midway Studio, where she shared space with Taft and other Chicago sculptors. In his groundbreaking *The History of American Sculpture,* Lorado Taft mentions Walker as a significant young sculptor and specifically refers to her Chief Keokuk statue.

Walker created both architectural and cemetery sculpture. She was a member of the National Sculpture Society and was inducted into the Iowa Women's Hall of Fame in 1987. Late in life, following the 1948 destruction of her Chicago studio, Walker moved to Colorado Springs, Colorado, where she occasionally modeled pottery for the Van Briggle Pottery company. She died there at age 99 in 1973.

Fred Ben Watkins
No information available; *fl.* 1968.

JERRY ALEXANDER

Jerry Alexander owns an equipment rental and sales company that handles aerial lifts. Begun in 1979, the family business fronts I-57 in Bourbonnais, Illinois. Wanting to place something in front of the business that would attract attention while expressing a sense of patriotism, Alexander thought a statue of Abraham Lincoln, whom he personally admires, would perfectly reflect his pride of country. After an internet search, he located FAST Corporation in Sparta, Wisconsin. He met with the owner, reached an agreement, and eight months later, *Abe* arrived. Installed on a ten-foot-high base elevating him to a height of twenty-nine feet, *Abe* continues to draw interest from local residents and travelers.

BRYON C. ANDREASEN

Bryon C. Andreasen is a Research Historian at the Abraham Lincoln Presidential Library and Museum in Springfield, Illinois. He earned a J.D. from Cornell University and formerly practiced law in New York. He earned a Ph.D. in History at the University of Illinois at Urbana-Champaign. He has taught at the University of Illinois and Illinois State University, and is the recipient of several awards for research and writing. He is a frequent participant at historical conferences and has published articles in several Civil War anthologies and reviews in *Civil War History*, *Journal of Illinois History*, *Journal of the Illinois State Historical Society*, *Western Historical Quarterly*, *Journal of the Abraham Lincoln Association*, *H-Net Reviews in the Humanities & Social Sciences*, and *Mormon Historical Studies*. His dissertation, "'As Good a Right to Pray': Copperhead Christians on the Northern Civil War Home Front," reveals an important and overlooked religious dimension to Democratic opposition to the Republican war effort. His duties at the Presidential Library and Museum include researching and writing rotating exhibitions, assisting the Illinois State Historian on various projects and conferences, and consulting on the State of Illinois's "Looking for Lincoln" Heritage Tourism Project. He is the editor of the *Journal of the Abraham Lincoln Association*. Bryon and his wife, Judy, reside near Springfield, Illinois, and are the parents of six children.

JEAN H. BAKER

Jean H. Baker is Elizabeth Todd Professor of History at Goucher College, Towson, Maryland, where she has taught since 1972. She received her B.A. from Goucher College, and her M.A. and Ph.D. from Johns Hopkins University.

A specialist in nineteenth-century political and cultural history, Baker is best known for her innovative look at cultural politics, *Affairs of Party*, and her definitive biography, *Mary Todd Lincoln: A Biography*. She wrote the introduction to the late Dr. C. A. Tripp's *The Intimate World of Abraham Lincoln*. Her current interest is in exploring the suffragist movement, resulting in *Sisters: The Lives of American Suffragists*.

Jean Taft Douglas Bandler

Jean Taft Douglas Bandler, daughter of Paul H. and Emily Taft Douglas and the granddaughter of sculptor Lorado Taft, was born in Illinois and has a lifetime interest in Abraham Lincoln. She graduated from the University of Chicago Laboratory Schools, as her mother had done, received her B.A. from Swarthmore College and her M.S.W. and D.S.W. at the Columbia University School of Social Work.

A social worker, she has worked in family agencies, done research on children's services, taught social welfare and social policy, and directed the undergraduate social work program at New York University. Active in civic affairs, she is a past president of Community Service Society in New York City, a founding member of the National Academy of Social Insurance, and a founder and past president of the Funeral Consumer Alliance of Connecticut. She lives in Bridgewater, Connecticut.

Paul J. Beaver

Paul J. Beaver was born on a farm west of Lincoln, Illinois, that was settled by his great-grandfather in the spring of 1853. This heritage sparked his interest in history in general, and in Abraham Lincoln and Logan County in particular.

Beaver attended Middletown Community High School and Lincoln College, where he earned his AA. He received his B.A. and M.A. (1964) degrees from Illinois State University in the fields of History and English. He has done additional study at Illinois State University in the Doctorate of Arts program. Beaver taught history and English for seven years at Elkhart Junior High School before joining the faculty at Lincoln College. For many years, he served as curator of the Lincoln Museum of Lincoln College. In 2004, the Lincoln College Board of Trustees awarded him the title of Professor Emeritus.

Beaver is a member of The Abraham Lincoln Association and was one of the founders of the Logan County Abraham Lincoln Heritage Foundation. He has frequently spoken about Abraham Lincoln in Logan County to Lincoln groups and Civil War round tables across the country. In 1983, Beaver published *The History of Logan County* and was co-editor of *The Pictorial History of Logan County*. He was also co-producer of the historical video *From Surveyor to President, Abraham Lincoln in Logan County*.

B. Irene Black

B. Irene Black was born in Lawrence County, Illinois, on December 28, 1911. She attended Fillmore Grade School and Bridgeport High School. On June 9, 1929, she married John Warren Black. They lived in Bridgeport, Illinois, where John was a coal and grain dealer and they raised two children. On their trip from Indiana to Illinois in the spring of 1830, the Lincoln family stayed with her ancestors at their farm on the White River in Pike County, Indiana.

Black is the founder of the Irene Black Historical and Genealogical Library in Bridgeport, which makes her large personal collection of historical and genealogical materials of the Lawrence County area available to the public. Over the past seventy-five years, she has been an active member and leader in various community and church organizations in Bridgeport. She has held leadership roles in the Daughters of the American Revolution, the Colonial Dames, and the National Genealogical Society. Black was a leader in persuading the State of Illinois to make needed repairs to the Lincoln Memorial at Westport, and the Memorial's support wall was recently rebuilt at her urging.

JERRY D. BLAKEMORE

Jerry D. Blakemore serves as the General Counsel for Southern Illinois University and as such is the chief legal officer for the University and its constituent institutions. Southern Illinois University is the second-largest public university in the state of Illinois.

Previously he served as the CEO and General Counsel of the Illinois Sports Facilities Authority, the municipal corporation responsible for the construction, maintenance, and operations of U.S. Cellular Field, home of the Chicago White Sox. Blakemore previously served as Managing Partner of Sales Goodloe Golden & Blakemore law firm where he headed the Regulatory and Governmental Affairs Practice Group.

At the age of 30, Blakemore served as Deputy Governor and Legal Counsel to former Illinois Governor James R. Thompson, making him the youngest Deputy Governor in Illinois history and the first African American. Blakemore's other public service positions include serving as Assistant Secretary for Public and Intergovernmental Affairs, Department of Labor, in the Reagan and Bush administrations; Commissioner on the Illinois Commerce Commission, and Chairman of the Illinois Board of Higher Education.

Blakemore is a graduate of Princeton University from which he received his B.A. in Political Science in 1976. Blakemore was the 1976 recipient of the Princeton University Frederick Douglass Award for his academic and community service achievements. Blakemore is a graduate of the John Marshall Law School in Chicago, Illinois and is licensed to practice law before the Illinois Supreme Court as well as the Federal District Trial and Appellate courts.

Blakemore's civic affiliations include: Past Chairman and member, Midwest Higher Education Commission; Past Vice Chairman and member of the Board of Directors of Chicago Communities in Schools, Inc., a not-for-profit agency which facilitates the provision of health, human and other community services to approximately fifty Chicago public schools. Blakemore serves as a Member of the Board of Directors of the Illinois Dollars for Scholars.

Justin A. Blandford

Justin A. Blandford is staff member of the Illinois Historic Preservation Agency. Prior to assuming his current role as Acting Superintendent of Historic Sites, he served for four years as the site manager for the Old State Capitol, Lincoln-Herndon Law Offices, and the Vachel Lindsay Home State Historic Sites. Justin, a graduate history student at the University of Illinois at Springfield, lives in Springfield with his wife, Holly Rae.

Gabor Boritt

Gabor Boritt was born and raised in Hungary and educated in South Dakota and Massachusetts. He served in Vietnam with the U.S. Air Force. He has been a loving mentor to a generation of students at Gettysburg College where he has served as the founder and director of the Civil War Institute, Fluhrer Professor of Civil War Studies, and co-founder and Chairman of the Board of Trustees of the Lincoln Prizes.

Boritt has held visiting appointments at the universities of Cambridge, Harvard, London, and Michigan. He is author, co-author, or editor of fifteen books on Lincoln and the Civil War, many of them Book of the Month Club and History Book Club selections. Boritt has received various awards, fellowships, an honorary degree, and has been selected distinguished alumnus of his undergraduate institution, Yankton College, and his graduate school, Boston University. His most recent book is *The Gettsyburg Gospel*. He lives on a farm outside of Gettysburg.

Roger D. Bridges

Roger D. Bridges is executive director emeritus of the Rutherford B. Hayes Presidential Center, which he directed from 1988 to 2003. Prior to that he was founding editor of the Lincoln Legal Papers and director of the Illinois State Historical Library in Springfield. He is past president of The Abraham Lincoln Association and a long-time board member. He has published numerous articles on Lincoln, slavery and civil rights, and Illinois history, and with Rodney Davis edited *Illinois: Its History and Legacy* (1984). He has taught history at Bradley University, the University of South Dakota, the University of Illinois at Springfield, Bowling Green State University, and Illinois State University. He holds a B.A. and M.A. from the University of Northern Iowa and the Ph.D. in History from the University of Illinois at Urbana-Champaign. Now retired, he is currently working on a book-length history of African Americans in Illinois through the nineteenth century.

Giovanni Bucci

See Giovanni Bucci's photograph and biography under the list of sculptors.

Willard Bunn

Willard Bunn was born at Springfield, Illinois, in 1943. Bunn graduated from Princeton University in 1966 with a degree in history. In 1968, he received his MBA from The Darden School at the University of Virginia. He is a descendant of a family heavily involved with Lincoln. His great-great-grandfather, Jacob Bunn, was Lincoln's friend and served as Mary Lincoln's banker after the assassination. Jacob's brother, John W. Bunn, was a good friend of Lincoln and contributed to his 1860 presidential campaign.

In 1968 Bunn began a forty-year banking career with Chemical Bank in New York. In 1986 he succeeded his father as the chairman of Springfield Marine Bank, one of the two banks Lincoln ever used (the other was Riggs Bank in Washington).

In 1992, Bunn became chairman and chief executive officer of Banc One Illinois Corporation which merged with Marine Bank, a position he held until his retirement on December 31, 1994. Bunn serves on the boards of various local and state business and civic organizations.

Michael Burlingame

Michael Burlingame received his B.A. from Princeton University and his Ph.D. from John Hopkins University. He is the May Buckley Sadowski '19 Professor Emeritus of History at Connecticut College where he taught from 1968 to 2001.

A former Woodrow Wilson Fellow and Fulbright Scholar, Burlingame devoted his scholarly energies to investigating the life and times of Lincoln, about whom he has published six books. The first, titled *The Inner World of Abraham Lincoln* (University of Illinois Press, 1994), has been described by reviewers as "a revelation," "a triumph," and "the most convincing portrait of Lincoln's personality to date." His second book, *An Oral History of Abraham Lincoln* (Southern Illinois University Press, 1996), won the Abraham Lincoln Association Award.

Burlingame's massive *Abraham Lincoln: A Life* appeared in two volumes in 2009. In 1997, he published *Inside Lincoln's White House: The Complete Civil War Diary of John Hay*. In 1998, he published *Lincoln Observed: Civil War Dispatches of Noah Brooks*; *Lincoln's Journalist: John Hay's Anonymous Writings for the Press 1860-1864;* and an expanded edition of Walter B. Stevens's *A Reporter's Lincoln*. He edited other books, including Ida Tarbell's interviews with people who knew Lincoln.

Burlingame is treasurer of the Connecticut Association of Scholars. He is also on the board of directors of The Abraham Lincoln Association and the Abraham Lincoln Institute of the Mid-Atlantic. He also serves on the board of advisors for the Abraham Lincoln Studies Center at Knox College, Galesburg, Illinois. In 1997, he received an honorary degree from Lincoln Memorial University.

ORVILLE VERNON BURTON

Orville Vernon Burton is University Distinguished Teacher/Scholar and Professor of History, African American Studies, and Sociology at the University of Illinois at Urbana-Champaign.

Burton's most recent book, *The Age of Lincoln*, was the recipient of the *Chicago Tribune's* 2007 Heartland Literary Award for nonfiction and a selection for Book of the Month Club, History Book Club, and Military Book Club.

Burton is also the author of more than a hundred articles and the author or editor of thirteen additional books, including: *The Essential Lincoln* and *In My Father's House Are Many Mansions: Family and Community in Edgefield, South Carolina*; *"A Gentleman and an Officer": A Military and Social History of James B. Griffin's Civil War*; and *The Free Flag of Cuba: The Lost Novel of Lucy Holcombe Pickens*.

In 1999, Burton was selected as the U.S. Research and Doctoral University Professor of the Year. He is also Director of the Institute for Computing in Humanities, Arts, and Social Science and Associate Director for Humanities and Social Sciences at the National Center for Supercomputing Applications, where he is a Senior Research Scientist.

Burton was born in Royston, Georgia and grew up in Ninety Six, South Carolina. He did his undergraduate studies at Furman University and received his Ph.D. from Princeton University.

DANIEL CAMERON

Daniel Cameron, 26, is a former news reporter for the Journal & Topics Newspapers, which covers a group of suburbs northwest of Chicago. While working on the *Niles Journal,* he developed a relationship with the staff at Village Hall, including Village Manager George Van Geem. Cameron particularly enjoyed working on personal, funny and unusual stories. So when Van Geem called him to say the statue of Lincoln that sits across from the village's police station was restored after being damaged under somewhat amusing circumstances, he didn't hesitate to look into the story.

Cameron is excited to be a part of this anthology honoring one of Illinois's greatest, Abraham Lincoln. He thinks it's especially appropriate to remember Lincoln now, as the nation turns its eyes toward another Illinois history-maker, Barack Obama. Cameron lives in northern Chicago.

JULIE CELLINI

Julie Cellini is chairman of the board of trustees of the Illinois Historic Preservation Agency and secretary of the board of the Abraham Lincoln Presidential Library Foundation. She served as chairman of the board of the Illinois State Historical Library and for twenty years has been a driving force in the creation and development of the Abraham Lincoln Presidential Library and Museum, a $150-million project that includes a research library, a history museum, a restored train station, an urban park, and a 620-car and bus parking garage—all located in Springfield's downtown historic district. She is involved in the Illinois Abraham Lincoln Bicentennial Commission and is co-chairman of the 150th anniversary commemoration of Oak Ridge Cemetery. She is a freelance writer and works on special projects for her family-owned real estate development company headquartered in Chicago. Cellini resides in Springfield, Illinois.

Guoxing Chai

Guoxing Chai is a Senior Vice President at the global bank HSBC. His specialty is in risk management and analytical solutions, particularly in managing emerging markets. He travels extensively to Latin America, Asia, Eastern Europe, and the Middle East. He previously worked for GE Capital in Consumer Finance and Commercial Insurance, with roles including Chief Credit Officer and Chief Operating Officer.

Chai has a B.A. degree in English Literature from Fudan University, China, and an MBA from the University of Illinois at Springfield. He came to the United States in 1988 with the generous help of a local attorney and a local doctor in Springfield.

He is married to Jian with two children, Aaron and Ashley.

Aaron Chai

Aaron Chai is a 13-year-old student at Woodlawn Middle School in Barrington, Illinois. He is on the Honor Roll. He is on the school basketball team and runs track and field. His grandfather trains him in basketball. He is currently learning two languages, Chinese and Spanish, both of which he thinks are going to be of use when he grows up.

He enjoys watching TV and playing with friends in his free time. He is an admirer of Lincoln and his work. He wants to be like his father and become a businessman when he grows up.

James M. Cornelius

James M. Cornelius received his B.A. in English from Lawrence University of Wisconsin and his M.A. and Ph.D. in history from the University of Illinois at Urbana-Champaign. He worked in the UI Library's fabulous Illinois History and Lincoln Collection for about eight years before coming to Springfield in May 2007. Earlier he worked as an editor in New York City at Doubleday, Random House, and *Collier's Encyclopedia.* He has written a number of books and dozens of articles and book reviews about American and British history, architecture, and baseball. As Curator of the Lincoln Collection at the Abraham Lincoln Presidential Library, he feels that he may have the best job in the United States.

Cullom Davis

Cullom Davis, a native of Central Illinois, is Professor Emeritus of History at the University of Illinois at Springfield. From 1988 to 2000, he was Director and Senior Editor of The Lincoln Legal Papers, which discovered over 100,000 legal records associated with Abraham Lincoln's quarter-century career as a lawyer. Its first product, *Law Practice of Abraham Lincoln, Complete Documentary Edition*, appeared in 2000.

Davis earned his B.A. at Princeton University, the M.A. and Ph.D. in American History from the University of Illinois, and Honorary Doctor of History degrees at Lincoln College (1999) and Knox College (2000). Davis is the author and editor of five other books, including *The Public and Private Lincoln* (1979), and numerous articles in American political history, Lincolniana, oral history, legal history, and Illinois history. His awards include the Lincoln Memorial University Diploma of Honor and several visiting faculty appointments, including a Fulbright research professorship. Davis has been president of The Abraham Lincoln Association, the Oral History Association, and the Association for Documentary Editing, and chairman of the Illinois Humanities Council. He serves as an advisor to both the Illinois and the United States commissions planning the Abraham Lincoln Bicentennial.

Robert J. and Patricia James Davis

Robert Davis, author of *A Soldier's Story,* recently retired as Fiscal Officer at the Illinois Department of Natural Resources, in Springfield, Illinois. He also worked for Deere & Company and in banking. He has taught at the University of Illinois at Springfield and Lincoln Land Community College in Illinois. Mr. Davis serves on the Board of Directors of The Abraham Lincoln Association, the Sangamon County Historical Society, and the Land of Lincoln Boy Scouts of America. He has been studying the Civil War for more than thirty years. He is well known as a Civil War re-enactor, particularly for his one-man presentation about an African-American soldier, Andrew Lewis, who served in the 29th Illinois Infantry, United States Colored Troops. He has made many presentations at schools and before various audiences including the Abraham Lincoln Presidential Library/Museum, the Sangamon County Historical Society, and the Quincy Cultural Festival – African American Heritage Program.

Robert Davis received his B.A. from Wayne State University, Detroit, Michigan; M.P.A. from Princeton University; and MBA from the University of Chicago.

Patricia James Davis has been involved in theater for a number of years. She portrayed Eva Monroe in *Time between Times,* a Phil Funkenbush original play, and currently performs as Rose Adams in "My Front Porch" at the Abraham Lincoln Presidential Museum. In addition, Patricia does civil war re-enactments of Mary Elizabeth Bowser, Susan King Taylor, Sojourner Truth, and Elizabeth Keckley. She has appeared as Calpurnia in *To Kill a Mockingbird* at the Barn Theater in Moline, Illinois; the Springfield Theater Center; and at the Sophie Leschin Theater in Jacksonville, Illinois. Other theater experiences include Stella in *Steal Away* at the Eastside Theater, Bess Delaney in *The Delaney Sisters, Having Our Say* at New Salem, and the Hoogland Center for the Performing Arts. She has done industrial training videos, commercial print and television ad campaigns. Mrs. Davis has an M.S.W. from the University of Iowa and is a counselor at the Southern Illinois University School of Medicine. In her spare time Patricia loves to play golf, read, ballroom dance, travel, and present etiquette workshops.

Patricia and her husband Robert reside in Springfield and are the proud parents of three children and five grandchildren.

RODNEY O. DAVIS

Rodney O. Davis, Szold Distinguished Service Professor Emeritus of History, began teaching American history at Knox College in 1963. He helped establish the American Studies program at Knox and for many years was its chairman. He received his B.S. in Journalism from the University of Kansas in 1954, M.A. in History from the University of Kansas in 1959, and Ph.D. in History from the University of Iowa in 1966.

Davis is a much-honored teacher, a specialist in nineteenth-century American history, and a recognized authority on the history of Illinois. A prize-winning essayist, his scholarly publications include articles on Lincoln, early Illinois politics, and editions of Thomas Ford's *A History of Illinois* (1995) and Ward Hill Lamon's *The Life of Abraham Lincoln*. He is co-editor, with Douglas L. Wilson, of a new edition of the Lincoln-Douglas debates and of *Herndon's Informants: Letters, Interviews and Statements About Abraham Lincoln* (1998). Other works include: "'Lincoln's 'Particular Friend' and Lincoln Biography," *Journal of the Abraham Lincoln Association* (1998); with Douglas L. Wilson, ed. *Herndon's Lincoln* (2006); and "The Frontier State, 1818-1848," with John M. Hoffmann, ed., *A Guide to the History of Illinois* (1991).

DAVID HERBERT DONALD

David Herbert Donald was born in 1920 at Goodman, Mississippi, and is a historian of the American Civil War. The Charles Warren Professor of American History (emeritus since 1991) at Harvard University, he specializes in the Civil War and Reconstruction periods, and in the history of the South. He has written over thirty books, including his biography of Abraham Lincoln, which has been praised by Eric Foner as the best biography of Lincoln. Other works include his Pulitzer-Prize-winning biographies of politician Charles Sumner and writer Thomas Wolfe, and his revision of the Randall textbook, *Civil War and Reconstruction* (1961, 2001).

Donald took his Ph.D. in 1945 under James G. Randall at the University of Illinois. He taught at Columbia University, Johns Hopkins and, from 1973, Harvard University. He also taught at Smith College, the University of North Wales, Princeton University, University College London, and served as Harmsworth Professor of American History at Oxford University. At Johns Hopkins, Columbia, and Harvard he trained dozens of graduate students. He received two Pulitzer Prizes, several honorary degrees, and served as president of the Southern Historical Association.

Donald's first book *Lincoln's Herndon* (1948) was a heavily researched and annotated and skillfully written biography of William Herndon, the junior partner in Abraham Lincoln's law firm in Springfield, Illinois.

WILLIAM M. DRAKE

William M. Drake is a Chicago architect and Illinois farmer. He was born in Chicago, but his family soon moved to his grandfather's farm on Elkhart Hill where he spent his childhood and formative years. He is a graduate of Harvard College and the Harvard Graduate School of Design and received a Ph.D. from Pacifica Graduate Institute. He lives on his farm in Elkhart and in Santa Fe, New Mexico.

His maternal great-great-grandfather was John Dean Gillett, who was known as "the cattle King of Illinois" for his prize-winning Shorthorn cattle which he grazed in the tallgrass prairie and exhibited and marketed at the Chicago Stockyards.

His great-grandfather, Richard J. Oglesby, a Civil War General, U.S. Senator (1861-4), and Governor of Illinois (1865-9 and 1885-9), was a close friend and supporter of President Lincoln.

Drake's grandfather, John B. Drake, was the original builder and owner of the Blackstone and the Drake Hotels in Chicago.

Richard J. Durbin

Richard Joseph "Dick" Durbin is currently the senior United States Senator from Illinois and Democratic Whip, the second highest position in the party leadership in the Senate. He became Majority Whip of the U.S. Senate when the 110th Congress convened on January 4, 2007.

Durbin was born on November 21, 1944, in East St. Louis where he graduated from Assumption High School in 1962. He earned a B.S. from the School of Foreign Service at Georgetown University in 1966 and his J.D. from Georgetown University Law Center in 1969. He was admitted to the Illinois bar later that year.

Upon graduation, Durbin opened a law practice in Springfield, Illinois. He served as legal counsel to Lieutenant Governor Paul Simon from 1969 to 1972, and then as legal counsel to the Illinois State Senate Judiciary Committee from 1972 to 1982. In 1982, Durbin won the Democratic nomination for the 20th Congressional District, which includes most of Springfield. He was re-elected six more times, rarely facing serious opposition.

Durbin became the Democratic Party's candidate for the Senate to replace the retiring Democratic incumbent, Paul Simon, in 1996. In April of 2006, *Time* Magazine listed Senator Durbin as one of America's 10 Best Senators.

Jim Edgar

Jim Edgar, a distinguished fellow with the Institute of Government and Public Affairs, University of Illinois at Urbana-Champaign, was the 38th governor of Illinois. Before becoming governor, Edgar served as secretary of state for 10 years and was elected to the Illinois House from Charleston in 1976. He received a B.A. in history from Eastern Illinois University in 1968.

As governor, he made fiscal discipline and children the cornerstones of his two terms. First elected in 1990, Governor Edgar won re-election in 1994 by the largest margin ever for a governor. His popularity as governor prompted a *Chicago Tribune* columnist to write near the end of his administration that Edgar's popularity in Illinois was "second only to Michael Jordan's."

Edgar has served in a variety of leadership roles, including president of the Council of State Governments, as a member of the executive committee of the National Governors' Association, and as chairman of the Midwest Governors' Association. He has also been a Resident Fellow at the John F. Kennedy School of Government at Harvard University. Governor Edgar serves on a variety of civic and corporate boards of directors.

Daniel Mark Epstein

Daniel Mark Epstein is a biographer, poet, and dramatist whose work has been widely published and performed. Born in Washington, D.C. in 1948, he was educated at Kenyon College. In the 1970s his poetry first appeared in *The New Yorker, The Atlantic Monthly,* and *The New Republic.* His first volume of poems was published by Liveright in 1973. His plays appeared soon thereafter in regional theater and Off-Broadway, and in 1978 he received the Prix de Rome for his poetry and dramatic works.

In the 1980s he wrote his first biography, *Sister Aimee: The Life of Aimee Semple McPherson*, now in its fourth printing. His biography *Nat King Cole* was a 1999 New York Times Notable Book, reviewed on the cover of the *New York Times Book Review,* and his biography of Edna St. Vincent Millay was a New York Public Library Honoree, "Books to Remember" for 2001. His honors include a National Endowment for the Arts fellowship in 1974, a Guggenheim Fellowship in 1984, and an Academy Award for Lifetime Achievement from the American Academy of Arts and Letters in 2006.

Other books are *The Traveler's Calendar* (2002) as well as a book of stories, *Star of Wonder* (1986) and the memoir *Love's Compass* (1990). His plays include *Jenny and the Phoenix, The Midnight Visitor,* and *The Leading Lady.* In 2005, Epstein wrote the libretto for *Jefferson & Poe: A Lyric Opera in Two Acts*—music by Damon Ferrante.

John Mack Faragher

John Mack Faragher is Arthur Unobskey Professor of History, Professor of American Studies, and Director of the Howard R. Lamar Center for the Study of Frontiers and Borders at Yale University. He was born in Phoenix, Arizona and raised in southern California. He attended the University of California, Riverside where he received a B.A. in 1967 and did social work, before coming to Yale to earn a Ph.D. in 1977. After fifteen years as a professor at Mount Holyoke College, he returned to Yale in 1993. His books include *Women and Men on the Overland Trail* (1979); *Sugar Creek: Life on the Illinois Prairie* (1986); *Daniel Boone: The Life and Legend of an American Pioneer* (1992); and *The American West: A New Interpretive History* (2000), with Robert V. Hine.

Andrew Ferguson

Andrew Ferguson is an American journalist and author. He is senior editor of *The Weekly Standard* and a columnist for *Bloomberg News* based in Washington, D.C. Before joining the *Standard* at its founding in 1995, he was senior editor at the *Washingtonian* magazine. He has been a columnist for *Fortune*, *TV Guide*, and *Forbes FYI*, and a contributing editor to *Time* magazine. He has also written for *The New Yorker*, *New York*, *The New Republic*, the *Los Angeles Times*, and the *Washington Post*. In 1992, he was a White House speechwriter for President George H. W. Bush. A collection of his essays, *Fool's Names, Fool's Faces*, was published in 1996, and *Land of Lincoln* was published in 2007.

Thomas R. Fitzgerald

A native Chicagoan, Thomas R. Fitzgerald attended Loyola University before enlisting in the United States Navy. Following his tour of duty in the Navy, he graduated with honors from The John Marshall Law School, where he was a founder of the school's current law review and served as the law review's associate editor.

The son of a circuit court judge, Justice Fitzgerald began his own career in the law as a prosecutor in the Cook County State's Attorney's Office. When first elected to the bench in 1976, he was the youngest Cook County Judge. He was elected to the Supreme Court of Illinois for the First District in 2000.

The Illinois Judges' Association honored him with the Lifetime Achievement Award in 2005. Justice Fitzgerald is a 2008 recipient of the Justice John Paul Stevens Award from the Chicago Bar Association. He is a member of the Leo High School Hall of Fame.

As a law professor, Justice Fitzgerald has taught at The John Marshall Law School and Chicago-Kent College of Law, where he was assistant coordinator of the trial advocacy program from 1986 to 1996. He also has taught at the Einstein Institute for Science, Health and the Courts. He was named an Honorary Science and Technology Fellow by ASTAR in 2006.

Justice Fitzgerald has served as president of the Illinois Judges' Association, chair of the Illinois Supreme Court Special Committee on Capital Cases, member of the Governor's Task Force on Crime and Corrections, chairman of several committees of the Illinois Judicial Conference, member of the Chicago Bar Association's Board of Managers, and past chairman of the Chicago Bar Association's committees on constitutional law and long-range planning. Justice Fitzgerald is a member of The John Marshall Law School Board of Trustees since 2005.

Guy C. Fraker

Guy C. Fraker is a graduate of the University of Illinois and has practiced law in Bloomington since 1962. A lifelong student of Abraham Lincoln's career on the circuit, Fraker has written extensively on the subject, spoken to a wide range of audiences, and guided tours of the Circuit on the roads that Lincoln traveled. He is a member of the Board of Directors of The Abraham Lincoln Association and the Advisory Committee to the National Abraham Lincoln Bicentennial Commission. He has practiced in the thirteen counties that constituted Lincoln's Eighth Circuit.

He has spoken on Lincoln in Central Illinois on numerous occasions to service clubs, college classes, and historical societies. He has made presentations to the Conference on Illinois History, Eureka College, Postville Courthouse in Lincoln, Illinois, and Illinois State University.

Doris Kearns Goodwin

Doris Kearns Goodwin was born in Brooklyn, New York, and grew up in Rockville Centre, New York. She received her B.A. from Colby College in 1964. She later earned a Ph.D. in government from Harvard University. She won a Woodrow Wilson Fellowship in 1964. Goodwin went to Washington, D.C., as a White House Fellow in 1967 during the Johnson administration, working as his assistant. After Johnson left office, she assisted the President in drafting his memoirs.

After LBJ's retirement in 1969, Goodwin taught government at Harvard for ten years, including a course on the American Presidency. In 1977, her first book was *Lyndon Johnson & the American Dream*, drawing on her conversations with the late president. This book became a *New York Times* bestseller and provided a launching pad for her literary career. Goodwin won the Pulitzer Prize in 1995 for *No Ordinary Time: Franklin and Eleanor Roosevelt: The American Homefront During World War II.* In 1998 Goodwin received an honorary LHD from Bates College. She won the 2005 Lincoln Prize (for best book about the American Civil War) for *Team of Rivals*, a book about Abraham Lincoln's Presidential Cabinet. She is currently a member of the Abraham Lincoln Bicentennial Commission advisory board. She lives in Concord, Massachusetts.

Allen C. Guelzo

Allen C. Guelzo is Henry R. Luce Professor of the Civil War Era and Professor of History at Gettysburg College. He is formerly Dean of the Templeton Honors College at Eastern University where he was the Grace F. Kea Professor of American History. Guelzo holds an M.A. and a Ph.D. in history from the University of Pennsylvania, an M.Div. from Philadelphia Theological Seminary, and an honorary doctorate in history from Lincoln College in Illinois.

Guelzo's essays, reviews, and articles have appeared in publications ranging from the *American Historical Review* and *The Wilson Quarterly* to newspapers such as *The Philadelphia Inquirer* and *The Wall Street Journal.* In 2000, his book *Abraham Lincoln: Redeemer President* won both the Lincoln Prize and the Abraham Lincoln Institute Prize, and in 2005, his book *Lincoln's Emancipation Proclamation: The End of Slavery in America* won both prizes again, making him the first double Lincoln Laureate in the history of both prizes. Guelzo's other publications include *Edwards on the Will: A Century of American Philosophical Debate*, *The Crisis of the American Republic: A New History of the Civil War and Reconstruction*, and an edition of Josiah G. Holland's *Life of Abraham Lincoln.* For the Teaching Company, he produced a twelve-part lecture series on Abraham Lincoln, which appeared in 2005 and is available on DVD.

Guelzo has received several teaching and writing awards, including the American Library Association Choice Award, The Albert C. Outler Prize in Ecumenical Church History, and the Dean's Award for Distinguished Graduate Teaching at the University of Pennsylvania.

Daniel Guillory

Daniel Guillory is Professor Emeritus of English at Millikin University, from where he retired in 2004. At Millikin, Guillory was named the Hardy Distinguished Professor of English (1984-1986 and 1994-96), Distinguished Faculty Lecturer (1989), and recipient of the Alpha Lambda Delta Teaching Award and Outstanding JMS Educator Award. He has published two books of regional essays: *Living With Lincoln* and *When the Waters Recede*; a book of poetry: *The Alligator Inventions*; and a work of photojournalism entitled *Images of America: Decatur*. Another work of photojournalism, *Wartime Decatur: 1832-1945*, and a sixth book, *Macon County*, appeared on January 29, 2007.

He has won awards from the Illinois Arts Council, the Academy of American Poets, the National Endowment for the Humanities, and the American Library Association. Dr. Guillory's poetry also appears in *Benchmark*, ed. by James McGowan, and in *Illinois Voices*, ed. by Kevin Stein. He is the author of the introduction to the reissue of *The Lemon Jelly Cake* by Madeline Babcock Smith and the introduction to *Tramping Across America* by Vachel Lindsay. His essay "Being Midwestern" appeared in *Essays From the Middle*, ed. by Becky Bradway. He recently published a new book called *The Lincoln Poems*.

Kathryn M. Harris

Kathryn M. Harris serves as Library Services Director at the Abraham Lincoln Presidential Library in Springfield, Illinois. She is active in library and history-related organizations including The Abraham Lincoln Association and the Illinois Library Association. She is active in her community and has received various awards including the Studs Terkel Humanities Service Award from the Illinois Humanities Council and the President's Award from the Springfield chapter of the NAACP. Kathryn enjoys acting and performance theatre and most especially enjoys introducing "Harriet Tubman" to library, school, and community groups.

Mark D. Hassakis

Mark D. Hassakis was born in Mt. Vernon, Illinois, on October 5, 1951. He received his B.A. from Northwestern University and his J.D. from St. Louis University School of Law. He was admitted to practice law in Illinois in 1976. Hassakis is a partner in Hassakis & Hassakis where he specializes in personal injury, workers' compensation and medical malpractice. He is a member and past president of the Jefferson County Bar Association. He is a member of the Chicago, Illinois State, and American Bar Associations; Hellenic Bar Association of Illinois; Illinois Trial Lawyers Association; and American Association for Justice. A member of the Board of Governors since 2002, he served on the Assembly from 1978 to 1984 and 1988 to 1994, and was president of the Illinois Bar Foundation from 2000 to 2002. He is in line to become its president in June 2010.

He is a director and past vice-president of Downtown Development Corporation of the City of Mt. Vernon. He was a founding member and past president of the Mt. Vernon West Rotary Club. He is a Friend of the Mitchell Museum, a member of the Lincoln Park Foundation and the Jefferson County Historical Society and a past director of Mt. Vernon Bright & Beautiful. He served on the Mt. Vernon Township High School Board of Education from 1978 to 1986.

Earl W. Henderson, Jr.

Earl W. Henderson, Jr. was born in Indiana in 1931. At about age nine, he moved with his parents to Springfield, Illinois. He attended Springfield High School and the University of Illinois, graduating with a B.A. in Architecture in 1954 and a MS in Architectural Engineering in 1959. Henderson served in the military during the Korean Conflict and thereafter worked for four years in Denver, Colorado.

In April 1961, he returned to Springfield and became the partner of Donald E. Ferry in the firm of Ferry and Henderson Architects, a partnership which endured for twenty-four years. The firm's over 400 projects varied in size and complexity, with the most rewarding being the reconstruction of the Old State Capitol in Springfield, Illinois. The successful completion of that project in 1968 was recognized as a cutting-edge event in restoration architecture, receiving several national and state professional awards.

Other restoration/preservation projects include the Lincoln Home in Springfield and the Iowa Territorial Capitol in Iowa City. Ferry and Henderson Architects also received numerous design awards for its contemporary design abilities for commercial, industrial, and educational projects.

Henderson has written articles for professional journals and has spoken to service clubs, university classes, and conferences on education. He has been a member and Chairman of the Springfield Historic Sites Commission and Chairman of the Capitol City Plan Commission. In 1976, Henderson served on the State of Illinois Commission to celebrate the nation's Bicentennial (1776–1976), and in 2008 served as an Advisor to the national Abraham Lincoln Bicentennial Commission. Since 1965, Henderson has been a member of the Board of Directors of The Abraham Lincoln Association.

John Hoffmann

John Hoffmann was born and raised in Springfield, Illinois. Hoffmann holds degrees from Swarthmore College and Harvard University and has written miscellaneous pieces on Lincoln, the Civil War, and Illinois history. Hoffmann is curator of the Illinois History and Lincoln Collections of the University of Illinois Library at Urbana-Champaign.

Harold Holzer

Harold Holzer is one of the country's leading authorities on Abraham Lincoln and the political culture of the Civil War era. A prolific writer and lecturer, and frequent guest on television, he serves as co-chairman of the National Abraham Lincoln Bicentennial Commission. Holzer currently serves as Senior Vice President for External Affairs at The Metropolitan Museum of Art in New York.

Holzer has authored, co-authored, or edited 30 books, including: *The Lincoln Image* (1984); *Changing the Lincoln Image* (1985); and *The Confederate Image* (1987), all with Mark E. Neely, Jr., and Gabor S. Boritt; *The Lincoln Family Album* (1990), *Mine Eyes Have Seen the Glory: The Civil War in Art* (1993), and *The Union Image* (2000) with Neely; and *Lincoln on Democracy*

(1990) with Mario M. Cuomo. His book *Lincoln At Cooper Union: The Speech That Made Abraham Lincoln President* (2004) won a 2005 Lincoln Prize, the most prestigious award in the field. In addition, Holzer has written more than 400 articles for both popular magazines and scholarly journals, including *Life Magazine*, *American Heritage* (where he serves as a Contributing Editor), *The Chicago Tribune*, *The New York Times*, and *The Los Angeles Times*.

From 1991-1996, Holzer served as president of the Lincoln Group of New York and on the board of directors of The Abraham Lincoln Association. He is founding vice chairman and a regular lecturer at The Lincoln Forum, which hosts an annual symposium each year in Gettysburg, and serves on the Board of Directors of the Ulysses S. Grant Association. In February 2006, Holzer was also named co-chairman of The New York State Lincoln Bicentennial Commission. He lives in Rye, New York.

William Howarth

William Howarth is a native of Springfield, Illinois. He joined the Princeton University faculty in 1966 after earning a B.A. from the University of Illinois and a Ph.D. from the University of Virginia. A popular lecturer and innovative teacher, his courses at Princeton ranged from Shakespeare to Joyce, pre-colonial America to postmodern fiction.

Howarth is an authority on Henry D. Thoreau, having produced such seminal studies as *The Literary Manuscripts of Henry D. Thoreau*, *The Book of Concord: Thoreau's Life as a Writer* and *Walking With Thoreau*. From 1972 to 1980, he served as editor in chief of the 25-volume *Writings of Henry D. Thoreau*. His other books include *Nature in American Life, The John McPhee Reader, The Book of Concord, Traveling the Trans-Canada,* and *Mountaineering in the Sierra Nevada*. He wrote more than ninety essays and reviews for major periodicals such as *The Washington Post, The New York Times,* and *Smithsonian*. For sixteen years he traveled and wrote for the National Geographic Society on history, literature, travel, and natural science. These field experiences led him to teach Princeton's first courses on literary geography, environmental history, American places, and the relations of race and place.

Daniel Walker Howe

Daniel Walker Howe, born January 10, 1937 in Ogden, Utah, is a historian of the early national period of American history and specializes in the intellectual and religious history of the United States. He is Rhodes Professor of American History Emeritus at Oxford University (England) and Professor of History Emeritus at the University of California at Los Angeles. He received the Pulitzer Prize for *What Hath God Wrought,* his most famous book. He was president of the Society for Historians of the Early American Republic in 2001 and is a Fellow of the Royal Historical Society.

Howe graduated from East High School in Denver, Colorado, and received his Bachelor of Arts at Harvard College, magna cum laude in American History and Literature in 1959, and his Ph.D. at University of California, Berkeley in 1966. Currently he resides in Sherman Oaks, California.

Jesse Jackson, Jr.

Jesse Louis Jackson, Jr. is a member of the United States House of Representatives for Illinois's 2nd congressional district. He is the son of activist and former presidential candidate Jesse Jackson. Born in Greenville, South Carolina, on March 11, 1965, he was educated at St. Albans School, Le Mans Academy, North Carolina Agricultural and Technical State University, and Chicago Theological Seminary. He holds a J.D. from the University of Illinois College of Law. Before entering the House, he was the national field director of the National Rainbow Coalition and a member of the Rainbow/PUSH Coalition. He is a member of the Congressional Black Caucus and a founding board member of the Apollo Alliance. He took his seat in the House after winning a special election in December 1995, following the conviction and subsequent resignation of Representative Mel Reynolds.

Ron J. Keller

Ron J. Keller is assistant professor of history and political science at Lincoln College in Lincoln, Illinois, and director and curator of the Lincoln College Museum. Keller earned his undergraduate and graduate degrees from Eastern Illinois University, and has taken courses at the University of Virginia. Keller is author of "That Which Congress So Nobly Began," in the book *Lincoln and Freedom*. He is a contributing author for the *Oxford Encyclopedia of African-American History*, and Congressional Quarterly's *The Essential Lincoln*. Keller serves as editor of *The Lincoln Newsletter*. He also co-wrote and co-produced the documentary *From Surveyor to President: A. Lincoln in Logan County*, which won a Special Citation of Achievement from the Lincoln Group of New York for the greatest contribution to the scholarship of Abraham Lincoln in 2004. He serves on the Advisory Committee of the National Abraham Lincoln Bicentennial Commission, on the Illinois Abraham Lincoln Bicentennial Commission, and as co-chair of the Abraham Lincoln Bicentennial Commission of Lincoln, Illinois. He is a member of the Board of Directors of The Abraham Lincoln Association.

Greg Koos

Greg Koos is Executive Director of the McLean County Museum of History. A life-long resident of Bloomington, he has written and edited numerous works relating to the county, its people, architecture, and culture.

Katherine Simons Kowa

Katherine Simons Kowa was born in Umitilla, Florida in 1936. She was raised in Duncan and Henry, Illinois, and graduated from Henry Senachwine High School. She received her B.S. from Millikin University in Decatur, Illinois, and taught physical education and humanities in the Decatur Public School System for eleven years. In 1969, she received an A.A. from Richland Community College.

Kowa is President of the Union Street Foundation, a not-for-profit charitable corporation, which she formed in 1995, to act as a catalyst in revitalizing the inner-city Decatur neighborhood, Old Kings Orchard. She was instrumental in building a Community Center there where thousands of children and families have been served. She acquired and demolished drug houses within the area. In the 1990s, she moved to Fort Myers, Florida, where she volunteered in the inner city, teaching art to children. In 2006, she moved to Newnan, Georgia where she now resides.

Marilyn Kushak

Marilyn Kushak is Chair of the Illinois Abraham Lincoln Bicentennial Commission. She earned a Bachelor's Degree in Business from Michigan State University and a Master's Degree in Education from the University of Illinois at Springfield.

She is the co-owner of Widow at Windsor Antiques and a Partner and Director of WMAY/WNNS/WQLZ/WYVR radio stations, where she has served as Vice President Sales/Marketing. Marilyn has also served as Regional Sales Manager for Control Data Corporation, Director of Business Operations and Marketing for Syntech International, Director of Region IV Career Guidance Center for the Illinois State Board of Education, and Director, Adult Education Pre-employment Training and Job Placement.

She is a member of the UIS Chancellor's Community Advisory Board; Past Chair of the National Association of Broadcasters Diversity Committee; and Past Chair, Greater Springfield Chamber of Commerce. She has served on the Greater Springfield Economic Development Council; Illinois State Council on Vocational Education; been involved in the Springfield Junior League; Children's Miracle Network; Women's Distance Festival Run; Reading is FUNdamental; and Springfield Road Runner's Club.

Ray LaHood

Raymond H. "Ray" LaHood was born on December 6, 1945. From 1995 to 2009 he was a Republican member of the United States House of Representatives, representing downstate Illinois's 18th congressional district. He has gained national notoriety, especially among C-SPAN viewers, as the presiding officer of more debates than any other member. Most notably, he presided over the impeachment vote against President Bill Clinton. He was born in Peoria, Illinois, and educated at Bradley University in Peoria, Illinois. LaHood was a teacher, the director of the Rock Island County Youth Services Bureau, an aide to Representatives Tom Railsback and Robert Michel, and a member of the Illinois House of Representatives before entering the U.S. House. LaHood served on the Appropriations Committee and Intelligence Committee. President Obama nominated him to be U.S. Secretary of Transportation.

Lewis E. Lehrman

Lewis E. Lehrman was born in Harrisburg, Pennsylvania, August 15, 1938. He received his B.A. at Yale University in 1960, after which he won a Carnegie Teaching Fellowship as instructor of history on the Yale faculty. Subsequently, he received his M.A. as a Woodrow Wilson Fellow from Harvard University. He also has been awarded honorary degrees from Babson College, Gettysburg College, Marymount University, and Thomas Aquinas College. Lehrman ran for Governor of New York in January 1982, losing narrowly to Mario Cuomo. In 2005, he was awarded the National Humanities Medal by President George W. Bush.

Lehrman has written books and articles on American history, Abraham Lincoln, Alexander Hamilton and other historical figures, national security, and economic and monetary policy. He has co-authored the book *Money and the Coming World Order*. He is the managing partner of the Gilder Lehrman Collection, a national resource of American historical documents, now on deposit at the New York Historical Society, where he is also a trustee. Lehrman is co-founder of the Lincoln Prize, given annually to the best scholarly work published on Abraham Lincoln and the Civil War. He is co-chairman of the Board of Advisors of the Gilder Lehrman Institute of American History, which promotes the teaching of history in American high schools and colleges through the use of original documents. Lehrman is a trustee of the Gilder Lehrman Center at Yale University for the Study of Slavery, Resistance, and Abolition, which gives the annual Frederick Douglass prize. He is chairman of The Lehrman Institute, a public policy research and grant-making foundation founded in 1972, which created The Lincoln Institute to promote the study of America's sixteenth president. He is presently Senior Partner, L. E. Lehrman & Co., an investment firm he established.

ROBERT J. LENZ

Robert J. Lenz has been engaged in the general practice of law in Bloomington-Normal, Illinois since 1963. He was educated at Freeport High School, Freeport, Illinois, the University of Illinois at Urbana-Champaign, and the University of Illinois College of Law. Lenz is a longtime amateur student of Abraham Lincoln and has made numerous appearances as a speaker on Abraham Lincoln. He is a vice president of The Abraham Lincoln Association and a member of The Lincoln Forum.

In addition to his interest in Lincoln, Lenz is a past president of the McLean County Bar Association and the David Davis Mansion Foundation. He has been a delegate to the North Atlantic Treaty Organization Conference in Istanbul, Turkey; a founding board member of the Adlai Stevenson Lectures; and an attendee at the 1971 YMCA International Committee World Meeting in Kampala, Uganda. From 1975 to 1981, Lenz served as a member of the Board of Trustees of the University of Illinois and he was president of the State of Illinois Universities Civil Service System, Merit Board. From 1979 to 1981 he was a member of the Illinois Board of Higher Education. Lenz lives on a small farm near the Mackinaw River on the border of Woodford and McLean Counties.

JOHN A. LUPTON

John Lupton was born in 1966 in Shelbyville, Illinois. He received his B.A. in history at Southern Illinois University at Carbondale in 1988 and M.A. in history at the University of Illinois at Springfield in 1992. Lupton is the Associate Director and Associate Editor of the Papers of Abraham Lincoln. He has been with the project since 1991. He has authored and co-edited numerous publications on Abraham Lincoln and the antebellum legal system and is a frequent speaker on those subjects. Lupton resides in Springfield, Illinois.

John W. McClarey

See John W. McClarey's photograph and biography under the list of sculptors.

Thomas Mallon

Thomas Mallon's seven novels include *Henry and Clara, Bandbox,* and the recently published *Fellow Travelers.* He has written non-fiction books about plagiarism (*Stolen Words*), diaries (*A Book of One's Own*), and the Kennedy assassination (*Mrs. Paine's Garage*), as well as two volumes of essays (*Rockets and Rodeos* and *In Fact*). His work appears in *The New Yorker, The Atlantic Monthly, The New York Times Book Review,* and other publications. He received his Ph.D. in English and American Literature from Harvard University and has taught at Vassar College, the George Washington University, and the Bread Loaf Writers' Conference. The recipient of Guggenheim and Rockefeller fellowships, as well as the National Book Critics Circle award for reviewing, he has been literary editor of *Gentlemen's Quarterly* and deputy chairman of the National Endowment for the Humanities. He lives in Washington, D. C.

R. Eden Martin

R. Eden Martin is counsel to the law firm Sidley Austin LLP. He was a partner from 1975 to 2004, and served as chairman of the firm's Management Committee from 1989 until 1999. Prior to becoming a partner, he was an associate at Sidley & Austin from 1967-1973, and served as inside general counsel of Arthur Andersen & Co. from 1973-1975. His law practice has centered on the representation of regulated industries and companies.

Martin is a member of the Boards of Directors of Nicor Inc. and Aon. He has served as president of The Commercial Club of Chicago and president of its Civic Committee since 1999. Among other civic and professional involvements, Martin is a fellow of the American Bar Foundation, a member of the Board of Directors of the Chicago Board Options Exchange, a life trustee of the Chicago Symphony Orchestra and the Ravinia Festival and a member of the Board of Trustees of Northwestern University and the Board of Directors of The Abraham Lincoln Association.

Jon Meacham

Jon Meacham was born in 1969. He is the editor of *Newsweek* magazine, a bestselling author, and a commentator on politics, history, and faith in America. Meacham began his journalistic career at the *Chattanooga Times*. He joined *Newsweek* as a writer in January 1995, became national affairs editor in June of that year, and was named managing editor in November 1998 at the tender age of twenty-nine. In September 2006, he was promoted to the position of Editor.

A *New York Times* bestselling author, Meacham is the author of *Franklin and Winston: An Intimate Portrait of an Epic Friendship* (2003), a chronicle of the wartime relationship between Roosevelt and Churchill, and *American Gospel: God, the Founding Fathers, and the Making of a Nation* (2006), a historical portrait of the spiritual foundation of America. He edited *Voices in Our Blood: America's Best on the Civil Rights Movement*, a collection of distinguished nonfiction about the mid-century struggle against Jim Crow. His biography *American Lion: Andrew Jackson in the White House* appeared in 2008. A contributing editor of *The Washington Monthly*, Meacham is a member of the Council on Foreign Relations and a communicant of St. Thomas Church Fifth Avenue, where he serves on the Vestry of the 180-year-old Episcopal parish. He is also a member of the Board of Regents of University of the South, the Vestry of Trinity Church Wall Street, the Leadership Council of the Harvard Divinity School, and the National Advisory Group of Washington National Cathedral. He received an honorary Doctor of Humane Letters degree from the Berkeley Divinity School at Yale University in 2005 and another from Loyola College in Maryland in 2007.

R. Dan Monroe

R. Dan Monroe is assistant professor of history at Millikin University in Decatur, Illinois. He earned a Ph.D. in history from the University of Illinois at Urbana-Champaign, where he worked with Professor Robert W. Johannsen. He received the Heiligenstein Award for Teaching Excellence and was a fellow at the Virginia Historical Society and Lincoln Legal Papers.

Monroe is the author of three books: *The Republican Vision of John Tyler* (2003), *At Home with Illinois' Governors: A Social History of the Illinois Executive Mansion* (2002), and *Shapers of the Great Debate on the Civil War: A Biographical Dictionary* (2005), with co-author Dr. Bruce Tap. He is currently working on his fourth book, a study of everyday life in the antebellum U.S. Monroe teaches a variety of courses at Millikin University, including his new course, "Abraham Lincoln in History and Film."

Jean Myers

Jean Myers is the site manager and curator of the Illinois Historic Preservation Agency's Metamora Courthouse State Historic Site, an 1845 Greek-Revival courthouse where Lincoln handled more than seventy cases, including two harboring slaves hearings and two murder cases. Myers is also the vice president of the Tri-County (Woodford, Tazewell, & Peoria) Abraham Lincoln Bicentennial Commission, chairperson of the Woodford County Historical Society Lincoln Statue Project, and co-founder of the Central Illinois Civil War Dance Society. He is also a retired counselor and emergency mental health services department head.

Barack Obama

Barack Obama was the junior United States Senator from Illinois and the fifth African-American senator in history when he was elected President on November 4, 2008, as a Democrat. Born August 4, 1961 to a Kenyan father and an American mother, Obama grew up in culturally diverse surroundings. He spent most of his childhood in Hawaii and lived for four years in Indonesia. After graduating from Columbia University and Harvard Law School, Obama worked as a community organizer, university lecturer, and civil rights lawyer before entering politics. He served in the Illinois Senate from 1997 to 2004 and the U.S. Senate from 2004 to 2008.

Obama delivered the keynote address at the 2004 Democratic National Convention while still an Illinois state legislator. He married in 1992 and has two daughters. He has authored two bestselling books: a memoir of his youth entitled *Dreams from My Father* and *The Audacity of Hope*, a personal commentary on U.S. politics.

LUKE O'BRIEN

Luke O'Brien is a freelance magazine journalist who lives in Washington, D.C. He grew up in a political family—his grandfather was an advisor to President John F. Kennedy; his father is a prominent lobbyist. O'Brien attended Harvard University, where he studied social anthropology and did research on the Hualapai Reservation in Arizona. After graduating, he worked in documentary film for National Geographic Television before moving to Clovis, New Mexico, for his first newspaper job. He received a master's degree in journalism in 2004 from Columbia University. His writing has appeared in *The New York Times, The Washington Post, Rolling Stone, Slate,* and many other publications.

JAMES A. PERCOCO

James A. Percoco has taught at West Springfield High School in Springfield, Virginia since 1980. The recipient of numerous education awards, Percoco was selected for the first *USA Today* All-USA Teacher Team in 1998 and named Outstanding Social Studies Teacher of the Year in 1993 at the Walt Disney Company American Teacher Awards. His first book, *A Passion for the Past: Creative Teaching of U.S. History* (1998), received the 2000 James Harvey Robinson Prize from the American Historical Association. From 1998-2004, Percoco served on the Board of Trustees for the National Council for History Education. An advocate for promoting good history education, Percoco has served as an educational consultant for the National Archives and Records Administration, where he received the Archivist's Award of Achievement in 1993, the National Gallery of Art, the National Park Service, the Vietnam Veterans Memorial Fund, and the Advisory Board of the Abraham Lincoln Bicentennial Commission.

In 1999 Percoco was selected by the United States Department of State to travel to Russia to work with Russian educators in a collaborative exchange. In December 2005, Percoco led a delegation of American history educators to Beijing, China to participate in a People-to-People Conference on education. His second book, *Divided We Stand: Teaching about Conflict in U.S. History,* was published in 2001. A third book, *My Summer with Lincoln,* was published in 2008. In 2004 Percoco was appointed an Adjunct Professor in Education at American University and was named by the University as History Educator-in-Residence.

MARK A. PLUMMER

Mark A. Plummer, Professor of History Emeritus at Illinois State University, is the author of *Lincoln's Rail-Splitter: Governor Richard J. Oglesby*. He also published *Peoria's Pagan Politician: Robert G. Ingersoll* and *Frontier Governor: Samuel J. Crawford of Kansas*. He has published a score of articles on nineteenth-century politics and politicians. His Ph.D. is from the University of Kansas. He has served as chairman of the history department at Illinois State University, as Fulbright Professor at National Taiwan University, and as president of the Illinois State Historical Society. He is a member of the Board of Directors of The Abraham Lincoln Association.

Glenn Poshard

Glenn Poshard is President of Southern Illinois University. He is the fifth of five children who grew up on a family farm in White County, Illinois. He graduated from Carmi Township High School in 1962 and after graduation served in the United States Army in Korea, where he received a commendation for outstanding service.

Dr. Poshard is a three-degree graduate of Southern Illinois University Carbondale, the first such graduate to serve on its Board of Trustees. Entering on the G.I. Bill, he earned a bachelor's degree in secondary education in 1970, a master's degree in health education in 1974, and a Ph.D. in higher education administration in 1984. While working toward his master's degree, Dr. Poshard taught and coached at Galatia and Thompsonville high schools.

In August 1984, Dr. Poshard was appointed to the Illinois State Senate. He was successfully elected later that year and was re-elected in 1986. The citizens of southern Illinois sent him to the United States Congress in 1989 to represent the 22nd Congressional District. He set a limit of ten years on his service in Congress and in 1998 won the Democratic nomination for Governor of the State of Illinois but lost in the general election. During his years in the Illinois Legislature and in the U.S. Congress, he advocated for campaign finance reform, clean coal research, the Shawnee National Forest, tourism, economic development, transportation, and higher education.

In 1999, Dr. Poshard and his wife, Jo, founded the Poshard Foundation, which raises money to fund care for abused, neglected, and abandoned children. The Foundation has been a leader in efforts to prevent child abuse throughout southern Illinois.

In 1999, Dr. Poshard was appointed Vice Chancellor for Administration for the Carbondale campus of Southern Illinois University, a post he held until July 2003. Governor Rod Blagojevich appointed him to the Board of Trustees of Southern Illinois University in January 2004. Later that year, he was elected Chair of the Board of Trustees, a position he held until declaring his candidacy for President of the University system.

The Poshard family includes two adult children, Dennis and Kristen, a daughter-in-law, Diane, and five grandchildren, Lydia, Madeline, America, Tucker, and Harrison. Glenn and Jo, a retired public school teacher, live in rural Murphysboro.

Shirley J. Portwood

Shirley J. Portwood graduated from Feitshans High School in Springfield, Illinois in 1963. She completed her Ph.D. in history at Washington University in St. Louis. She is currently a Professor in the Department of Historical Studies at Southern Illinois University at Edwardsville where she teaches history, including courses on African-American Community History, African Americans in Illinois, and African-American Women. Portwood's current research is on blacks in Illinois politics in the post-Reconstruction era. She is the author of *Tell Us A Story: An African-American Family in the Heartland,* a collection of African-American autobiography and family history set in Springfield and in rural southern Illinois, Missouri, and Arkansas from the 1920s through the 1950s.

Barbara Sancken

Barbara Sancken was born on February 10, 1933, at Pontiac, Illinois. She attended St. Mary's Catholic Grade School and graduated from Pontiac Township High School in 1951. After marrying Howard Sancken on January 26, 1952, she left the city for the farm, learning how to help with the dairy cows, drive a tractor, disc with harrow attached, haul in and elevate corn and soybeans, and live without plumbing the first four years. She is the mother of four children, two of whom have been lost to cancer, grandmother of six and great-grandmother of eight.

Sancken served as secretary-treasurer of the Owego School District for many years; two years as township trustee, eight years as township clerk, sixteen years as township supervisor and has been a member of the Livingston County Regional Plan Commission, presently serving as secretary-treasurer. She also serves on her church's finance council. After joining the *Pontiac Daily Leader* in 1965, Sancken worked as a reporter, photographer, feature writer, copy editor, and occasionally pasted up pages. She has won several first place Illinois Associated Press awards (two of them also Sweepstakes awards) in special edition, investigative reporting and spot news and, in 1982, a first place national AP award. In 1983, she won the National Headlines Award. Although retired from the newspaper in 1996, Sancken continues to write three columns weekly, bringing forth the Lincoln history, which resulted in the Lincoln statue featured in this work.

Diane Schaefer

Diane Schaefer lives on Lincoln Avenue in a quaint New England town along with her husband, teenage daughter, cocker spaniel, and two cats. She has been involved in fund raising for numerous nonprofit organizations and is currently an associate director with the University of New Hampshire Foundation. She is a direct descendant of F. W. Ingmire, a photographer in Springfield, Illinois, during the Civil War. Ingmire is perhaps most famous for his photographs of Lincoln's dog, Fido.

Thomas F. Schwartz

Thomas F. Schwartz is a native of Illinois, having spent his youth in Downers Grove. He attended the University of Illinois, Urbana-Champaign where he received the A.B., A.M. and Ph.D. in history and international relations. He became curator of the Henry Horner Lincoln Collection at the Illinois State Historical Library in 1985 and is an acknowledged authority on the sixteenth president and his times.

Schwartz is author of over one hundred articles, reviews, chapters, and electronic reference entries and editor of *"For a Vast Future Also": Essays from the Journal of the Abraham Lincoln Association* (1999). On November 19, 1993, Governor Jim Edgar named Schwartz to fill the post of State Historian, making him, at thirty-eight, the youngest person to serve in that position. With John Rhodehamel of the Henry Huntington Library, Schwartz co-curated the nationally acclaimed exhibition, *"The Last Best Hope of Earth": Abraham Lincoln and the Promise of America.* He has served as a historical consultant for numerous documentaries and has appeared on the *Today Show, Good Morning America, CBS Sunday Morning*, the History Channel, the Voice of America, and C-SPAN. He is senior editor of the *Journal of the Abraham Lincoln Association*, historical advisor for the *Journal of Illinois History,* and serves on a number of boards and commissions dealing with history, education, and culture. He continues as State Historian overseeing Research Collections including the Papers of Abraham Lincoln at the Abraham Lincoln Presidential Library in Springfield, Illinois. In addition, he is the chief historian for exhibits and content in the Abraham Lincoln Presidential Museum. Schwartz is also on the The Board of Directors of The Abraham Lincoln Association and advisory board for the state and federal Abraham Lincoln Bicentennial Commissions.

William G. and Mary F. Shepherd

William Shepherd is an Illinois lawyer whose practice concentrates in legislative and regulatory law. He is a member of the Board of Directors of the Abraham Lincoln Association.

Mary Farmer Shepherd is the Executive Assistant for the Abraham Lincoln Association. She has a B.S. in Finance from the University of Illinois and an MBA from Loyola University of Chicago.

Scott Simon

Scott Simon, NPR's Peabody-Award-winning correspondent, is the host of *Weekend Edition Saturday.* Simon joined NPR in 1977 as chief of its Chicago bureau. Since then, he has reported from all fifty states, covered presidential campaigns and eight wars, and reported from Central America, Africa, India, the Middle East, and the Caribbean.

The son of comedian Ernie Simon and actress Patricia Lyons, Simon grew up in Chicago, New York, San Francisco, Los Angeles, Montreal, Cleveland, and Washington, D.C. He attended the University of Chicago and McGill University, and he has received a number of honorary degrees.

Simon has received numerous honors for his reporting, including the Overseas Press Club and Alfred I. duPont-Columbia University Awards. Simon has been a frequent guest host of the CBS television program *Nightwatch* and CNBC's *Talk Back Live.* In addition to hosting *Weekend Edition Saturday*, Simon has appeared as an essayist and commentator on NBC's *Weekend Today* and *NOW* with Bill Moyers. He also narrated the documentary film "Lincoln of Illinois" for PBS. Simon has written for *The New York Times Book Review* and Opinion sections, the *Wall Street Journal* opinion page, *The Los Angeles Times*, and *Gourmet Magazine*. Simon's book *Home and Away: Memoir of a Fan* was published in 2000. His second book, *Jackie Robinson and the Integration of Baseball*, was published in 2002. Simon's first novel, *Pretty Birds,* was released in 2005.

Brooks D. Simpson

Brooks D. Simpson is Professor of History and Humanities at Arizona State University. He is author of several books on the Civil War and Reconstruction era including: *Let Us Have Peace: Ulysses S. Grant and the Politics of War and Reconstruction, 1861-1868*; *The Political Education of Henry Adams*, *America's Civil War*; *The Reconstruction Presidents*; and *Ulysses S. Grant: Triumph Over Adversity, 1822-1865*. Simpson has edited a volume of Abraham Lincoln's letters and speeches, a volume of letters of advice to Andrew Johnson, and a volume of William T. Sherman's letters. He is currently working on the second and final volume of his biography of Ulysses S. Grant.

Nancy Bliss Slepicka

Nancy Bliss Slepicka, community journalist, was the fourth-generation publisher of *The Montgomery County News.* Charles Wesley Bliss purchased the Hillsboro newspaper in 1892 and it was subsequently operated by his son, Clinton P. Bliss, his grandsons, Thomas and Robert Bliss, and his great-granddaughter, Nancy, and her husband, Richard.

In 2004, the business was merged with the town's other family-owned newspaper, *The Hillsboro Journal.* Nancy and Richard worked as senior editors of *The Journal-News* until retiring in 2007. She continues to contribute photo-features and opinion columns for *The Journal-News* and is a news correspondent for *The State Journal-Register* in Springfield.

Nancy is a former board member of the Illinois Press Association and former president and board member of both the International Society of Weekly Newspaper Editors and the Southern Illinois Editorial Association. In 2001 she was named a Master Editor and joined her father, Bob, and uncle, Tom, in the Journalism Hall of Fame at Southern Illinois University, Carbondale.

Ronald Spears

Ronald Spears of Taylorville, Illinois, is the Resident Circuit Judge for Christian County, Illinois, in the Fourth Judicial Circuit. He graduated from the University of Illinois in 1974 and from Southern Illinois University School of Law in 1977, where he served as editor-in-chief of the law review. From 1977 until 1979, Spears served as Law Clerk for Judge J. Waldo Ackerman in the United States District Court in Springfield, Illinois. In 1979, Spears joined the Taylorville law firm of Miley, Meyer & Austin, where he was engaged in the general practice of law, with emphasis on litigation in state and federal courts. He continued to practice law until the Illinois Supreme Court appointed him to the Circuit Court in 1993. Spears has presided over civil and criminal cases, bench, and jury trials throughout the nine-county Fourth Judicial Circuit. He serves as a mentor for new judges, has served on the Supreme Court Committee on Judicial Conduct, and is presently on the Illinois Judicial Conference Committee on Education for judges.

Spears has published articles on legal subjects and served on the teaching faculty for seminars for lawyers and judges on various legal topics. He is active in the Illinois State Bar Association. He is second vice president of the Illinois Judges Association and immediate past-president of the Lincoln-Douglas American Inn of Court. He is also a member of the American Bar Association and local bar associations. Spears has been active in numerous community, public service, and church activities. He served over thirty-four years in the Illinois Army National Guard, where he retired as a Colonel in the Judge Advocate General's Corps and a Certified Military Judge.

Kevin T. Stein

Kevin T. Stein is the Caterpillar Professor of English at Bradley University, Peoria, Illinois. Since December 11, 2003, Stein has served as Illinois Poet Laureate. He has received numerous awards for his poetry, including the 1987 Frederick Brock Prize awarded by *Poetry* magazine, the 1991 National Endowment for the Arts Poetry Fellowship, the 1992 Devins Award for Poetry, and the 1998 Indiana Review Poetry Award. In 2001 he was nominated for the Pulitzer Prize. Stein is the author of nine books of poetry and literary criticism, including the collection *American Ghost Roses* (2005), winner of the Society of Midland Authors Poetry Award. Among his work related to Illinois are the poetry anthology *Illinois Voices: An Anthology of Twentieth Century Poetry* (2001), co-edited with G. E. Murray, and the audio CD anthology *Bread & Steel: Illinois Poets Reading from Their Works.*

Adlai E. Stevenson III

Adlai Ewing Stevenson III, great-grandson of vice president Adlai Ewing Stevenson, was born in Chicago, Illinois, on October 10, 1930. He attended grammar schools in Illinois and Milton Academy, Massachusetts. He graduated from Harvard College in 1952, and from the law department of the same university in 1957. He entered the United States Marine Corps as a private in 1952, served as a tank platoon commander in Korea and was discharged as a first lieutenant in 1954 and from the Reserves in 1961 with the rank of captain. Stevenson was admitted to the bar in 1957 and commenced practice in Chicago. He served in the Illinois House of Representatives from 1965 to 1967 and as Treasurer for the State of Illinois from 1967 to 1970. On November 3, 1970, Stevenson was elected as a Democrat to the United States Senate to fill the unexpired term caused by the death of United States Senator Everett M. Dirksen. He was re-elected in 1974, and served from November 17, 1970, to January 3, 1981. Stevenson ran unsuccessfully as the Democratic candidate for governor of Illinois in 1982 and 1986. In 1992, he founded and served as chairman of the investment banking firm of SCM Investment Management. He is a resident of Hanover, Illinois.

Daniel W. Stowell

Daniel W. Stowell is the director and editor of the Papers of Abraham Lincoln. Stowell received his B.A. and M.A. from the University of Georgia, and his Ph.D. in American History from the University of Florida. After joining the staff of the Lincoln Legal Papers in 1996, Stowell became the director in 2000, and managed its expansion into the Papers of Abraham Lincoln. Stowell is the author or editor of five books, including *The Papers of Abraham Lincoln: Legal Documents and Cases* (4 vols., 2008), *Rebuilding Zion: The Religious Reconstruction of the South, 1863-1877* (1998), and *In Tender Consideration: Women, Families, and the Law in Abraham Lincoln's Illinois* (2002).

Nicky Stratton

Nicky Stratton retired in the fall of 2003 after 13 years as the Executive Director of the Springfield Convention & Visitors Bureau. Immediately following her retirement, she became the Director of the Looking for Lincoln Heritage Coalition (LFLHC), a not-for-profit organization, that works with communities and sites to help them enhance and market their Lincoln-related historic attractions. Before her retirement, Stratton was Chairman of the LFLHC Board of Directors for five years. In February 2008, Stratton stepped down from the position of Director to accept a less strenuous role as Associate Director. In that capacity she will continue to manage individual projects. Earlier, she spent seven years as the Director of Sales and Marketing for the Springfield Convetion and Visitors Bureau. Previous to that she was Director of Convention Services and Director of Tourism. Stratton is past Chair of Visit Illinois, Inc. and has twice served as the Chair of the Governor's Conference on Tourism.

She has served on committees for the National Tour Association, the American Bus Association, and the Illinois Society of Association Executives. She has been an active board member of the Illinois Council of Convention & Visitors Bureau and has participated as a workshop presenter and committee chair for the International Association of Convention and Visitors Bureau. She has also served on the boards of the Red Cross, the Springfield Art Association, the Salvation Army, the Iles House Foundation, the Great American People Show, Downtown Springfield, Inc., The Abraham Lincoln Association, and the Illinois Bicentennial Commission as well as the Springfield Bicentennial Committee.

Robert A. Stuart, Jr.

Robert Stuart, Jr. is a partner in Brown Hay & Stephens, which was founded by his great-great-grandfather John Todd Stuart in 1828, the oldest law firm in the state of Illinois. He is a fellow of the American College of Trust and Estate Counsel and of the American Bar Foundation as well as advisor to Leading Lawyers Network. In Springfield, he has chaired the Chamber of Commerce, the United Way Campaigns and the United Way Foundation. He is the Secretary/General Counsel of the National Recreation Foundation, Treasurer of the Abraham Lincoln Association, and Trustee of the Illinois State Museum Society. A past president of the Boy Scout Council, he holds the silver beaver and distinguished eagle awards. For service in masonry, he has been awarded the 33rd degree. The Illinois Association of Park Districts recently presented him its lifetime appreciation award.

Stuart has been Rotary club president, district governor and one of 17 directors on the board of Rotary International. He currently chairs Rotary International's constitution and bylaws committee and is raising funds for Rotary's 7 global Peace Centers. He has immunized children in Rotary's campaign to eradicate polio, opened water wells, delivered wheelchairs, dedicated new schools following the 2004 tsunami, and worked with clubs along the Gulf Coast in post Katrina-relief efforts. The Rotary Foundation has awarded him its Citation for Meritorious Service. Stuart has served as trustee and elder in his church. He and his wife live in Springfield, Illinois.

Louise Taper

Louise Taper is a historian and collector of Abraham Lincoln artifacts. She created the exhibition *The Last Best Hope of Earth: Abraham Lincoln and the Promise of America* which was at the Huntington Library from 1993-1994 and at the Chicago Historical Society from 1996-1997. She also served as an historical consultant for the television mini-series *Sandburg's Lincoln*. She is co-author of the book *Right or Wrong, God Judge Me: The Writings of John Wilkes Booth*, published by the University of Illinois Press. She serves on the boards of the Abraham Lincoln Association, the Abraham Lincoln Presidential Library and Museum Foundation, the Lincoln Forum, the Lincoln Legal Papers, and the Lincoln Prize at Gettysburg College. She is also a trustee of Lincoln College. She created the Taper collection which was purchased by the Abraham Lincoln Presidential Library and Museum in 2007.

Roger L. Taylor

Roger L. Taylor came to his current position as President of Knox College through an unusual route. After graduating from Knox—where he met his wife Anne (Zweifel)—he served in the United States Navy (including a year in Vietnam), received a law degree from Northwestern University and practiced law in Chicago for 30 years with the firm of Kirkland & Ellis. He then retired to his family farm south of Galesburg.

In September 2001, leaving his position as chairman of the Knox Board of Trustees, he agreed to serve temporarily as interim president. "Hire Roger" buttons began appearing on campus, and in February 2002, he was selected as Knox's 18th president.

Accessibility and enthusiasm have characterized Taylor's time at Knox. He moved his office from the corner of Old Main to a small hallway office. He and Anne—also a Northwestern-educated lawyer, who serves as volunteer Pro Bono Counsel for Knox—regularly eat lunch with students in the cafeteria and make it a point to attend student performances and athletic events. Taylor stops prospective students who are visiting campus to introduce himself and extol the virtues of a Knox education.

Next to talking with students, Taylor says that his favorite activity is taking the current Knox story to other alumni. "I've lost track of how many alumni tell me that Knox changed their lives. There is an enormous reservoir of good will among our alumni. I want to tell my fellow alumni how Knox still changes lives."

Taylor has set three goals for his tenure as Knox's president: "Nurturing academic excellence—Strengthening institutional self-confidence—Charting a course toward financial impregnability."

James R. Thompson

James R. Thompson, Illinois's longest-serving governor (1977-1991), is chairman of the law firm of Winston & Strawn, headquartered in Chicago. Thompson was educated at the University of Illinois and Washington University and received his law degree from Northwestern University Law School. He first joined Winston & Strawn in 1975 and then rejoined the firm as a partner when he left the governor's office in 1991. From 1959 to 1964, he served in the Cook County state's attorney's office, where he argued criminal civil rights cases before the Illinois and U.S. Supreme Courts. He then taught at the Northwestern Law School. In 1971, he became U.S. Attorney for the Northern District, where he established a solid reputation for prosecuting corrupt public officials. He is a member of the Illinois Bar. Thompson is also a director of FMC Corporation, FMC Technologies, Inc., the Chicago Board of Trade, Hollinger International (publisher of the *Chicago Sun-Times*), Prime Retail Inc., Prime Group Realty Trust, Navigant Consulting Group, Public Review Board HEREIU, Japan Society (New York), and MAXIMUS, Inc. He served on the American Bar Association Commission on Separation of Powers and Judicial Independence from 1996-1997. He was also a member of the National Commission on Terrorist Attacks upon the United States.

Timothy P. Townsend

Timothy P. Townsend is the historian at The Lincoln Home National Historic Site in Springfield, Illinois. He earned his B.A. in history from St. Ambrose University in Davenport, Iowa, and holds an M.A. in history from the University of Illinois at Springfield. Townsend serves as Chair of the Historic Sites Committee of the Lincoln States Bicentennial Task Force, on the National Abraham Lincoln Bicentennial Commission's Education Advisory Committee, on The Abraham Lincoln Association Board of Directors, on the Illinois State Historical Society Board of Directors and on the Lincoln Forum Board of Advisors. Tim regularly speaks for professional conferences and civic and community groups and has written the Lincoln home portion of the recently published *Abraham Lincoln: A Living Legacy; A Guide to Three Abraham Lincoln National Park Sites*. Townsend lives in Springfield with his wife Diane and their five children.

N. Ronald Thunman

Admiral Thunman attended the University of Illinois, College of Civil Engineering, and received his Bachelor of Science from the U. S. Naval Academy. After entering active duty, he successfully completed Submarine School, Nuclear Power School, and Nuclear Prototype Training. Additionally, he has been awarded two honorary doctoral degrees.

Adm. Thunman, during 35 years of active duty in the US Navy, served with distinction in numerous professional fields ranging from submarine duty, nuclear power, personnel management, education and training and research and development. As Deputy Chief of Naval Operations for Submarine Warfare (OP-02) and Chief of Naval Education and Training (CNET), he was responsible for implementation of major new program initiatives. As OP-02, he determined requirements and directed all programs involving submarines and submarine support and managed the planning and execution of an $18-billion annual budget. He has served numerous tours aboard submarines, including as commanding officer, and has served as the Commander Submarine Force, U.S. Pacific Fleet with fifty nuclear attack submarines and ten Polaris strategic submarines under his command.

Following retirement from the Navy, Adm. Thunman has held several significant positions in private industry, including the Chairman of the Board of Pinkerton Government Services Inc., an internationally recognized corporation which provides security services nationwide, and Vice Chairman of the Board of Illinois Bank Corporation of Springfield, Illinois. Other notable positions since his retirement from active duty include Chairman of the Board and CEO of CAE Electronics Inc., a world leader in the design of automated ship control systems and military system trainers, Chairman of the Board of ABB Government Services, and President and CEO of Valley Forge Military Academy and College. He holds the Navy Distinguished Service Medal (two awards) and Legion of Merit (four awards).

He currently serves as President of the Board of Advisors, U.S. Naval Submarine League, Board of Trustees, U. S. Naval Academy Foundation, and the U.S. Navy League.

Owsley Brown Thunman

Owsley Brown Thunman was born in Springfield. She attended high school and college in the East. She has one daughter, Allison. Owsley is an Episcopalian. She is a voracious reader. She loves music, the arts and travel. She says she is "artsy." She volunteers for civic and cultural organizations, and is a life member of the Illinois Symphony Orchestra Board of Advisors.

She also says that both political parties are represented in her household. Guess who is the liberal Democrat and who is the conservative Republican. It makes for interesting dinner conversation. Owsley is charming and fun.

Owsley will not tell you this, but it is interesting, particularly since you will be here for Lincoln's Birthday. She is the grand daughter of Christopher Columbus Brown, who was a clerk in the Lincoln law office in Springfield. Lincoln examined C. C. Brown for the bar and recommended his admission.

Carl Volkmann

Carl Volkmann was born and raised in Toluca, Illinois, and attended the public schools in this Central Illinois community. He graduated from Wartburg College with a B.A. in 1955 and from Wartburg Seminary with a Master of Divinity degree in 1959.

Carl and his family moved to Springfield in 1960, and he started his professional career as a high school history teacher. His focus changed from teaching to librarianship in the 1960s, and he received his MLS from the University of Illinois in 1969.

In 1970, he started working at Lincoln Library, the public library of Springfield, Illinois, as the Young Adult Librarian. He was appointed Assistant Director in 1972 and Library Director in 1981. He retired from Lincoln Library in 1993 and currently devotes his time to freelance writing and community volunteering. His many volunteer activities include a term as president of the Sangamon County Historical Society. Carl and his wife Roberta are the authors of *Springfield's Sculptures, Monuments and Plaques.*

Lexi Wallace

Lexi Wallace is a seventeen-year-old high school senior from Phoenix, Arizona. Wallace has always had a love of American history, and in the summer of 2008, she was a finalist in Now Debate This, a national scholarship competition that revolved around the question, "Who was the better president: George Washington or Abraham Lincoln?" Apart from history, Lexi has a true passion for art, music, and guitar and finds her greatest joy in serving the community through Key Club. For all her life, she has been described as the intelligent, yet remarkably quiet girl, yet would prefer to allow a witty man by the name of Abraham Lincoln to explain her reserved manner: "Better to remain silent and be thought a fool than to speak out and remove all doubt."

Daniel R. Weinberg

Daniel R. Weinberg has been president and sole owner of the Abraham Lincoln Book Shop, Inc. since 1984, having previously been co-owner since 1971. Since 1938, this firm has an international reputation as experts in the buying, selling, appraisal, and authentication of historical, literary, artistic, and museum properties. Weinberg pursued his undergraduate work, in history, at Temple University, Philadelphia, and his graduate work, in the same field, at New York University, New York City.

Weinberg has performed special research assignments for such institutions as The Lincoln Museum, Fort Wayne, Indiana; the Lincoln Heritage Museum at Lincoln College, the American Bar Foundation, Brandies University, University of Virginia, WTTW Channel 11 in Chicago, the Chicago Historical Society, the Chicago Public Library, the Chicago Bar Association, the ACLU. He has delivered numerous talks on the collecting and value of books and manuscripts as well as determining authenticity of historical documents.

Weinberg is a member of numerous historical societies and associations and currently, serves as a director of the Lincoln Forum, The Abraham Lincoln Association, and the Lincoln Group of Wisconsin. He is the executive vice president of the Professional Autograph Dealers Association and a member of the official Advisory Committee to the Federal Abraham Lincoln Bicentennial Commission. He serves on both the Board of Trustees and the Executive Board for Lincoln College, Lincoln, Illinois. He is co-author of *Lincoln's Assassins: Their trial and execution (2001)* and has lectured extensively on the subject. He has appeared on C-Span, the History Channel, WTTW Channel 11 in Chicago, and CBS-TV in Chicago.

Marnie Lanphier Wengren

Marnie Lanphier Wengren was born Margaret Lanphier in Springfield in 1916. Her father, Robert Carr Lanphier, and Jacob Bunn founded Sangamo Electric Company. She attended "Miss Elsie Logan's Little School for Individual Instruction," where eight little girls were taught the three Rs and French in one room of the Episcopal church Parish House. For two years, she attended Lawrence School where she won the DAR history medal. She went on to study at Masters School and Vassar. In 1938, she married Charles DeWitt Smith, then a graduate student in mine engineering, with whom she had four children. Her second marriage was to Richard Wengren. She has lived in metropolitan New York for four years and Lincoln, Massachusetts in suburban Boston. She began work in the Education Department of the Boston Museum of Fine Arts, and also trained there through forty years of learning the collections as Gallery Instructor. She was very involved at DeCordova in Lincoln, a contemporary art museum and sculpture park, serving as Chair of Board of Trustees there as well as Acting Director for two years. She has fourteen grandchildren and eleven great-grandchildren and currently lives in Lexington, Massachusetts.

B. Joseph White

B. Joseph White was born in Detroit in 1947 and raised in Kalamazoo, Michigan. In 2004, White was named the sixteenth president of the University of Illinois with its three campuses and 70,000 students. White graduated from the Georgetown University School of Foreign Service in 1969. He earned an MBA from Harvard Business School and a doctorate in business administration from the University of Michigan in 1975.

White was a professor of organizational behavior and industrial relations at Michigan. From 1981 to 1987, he was at Cummins Inc. in Columbus, Indiana, first as vice president for management development and then as vice president for personnel and public affairs. In 1991, he returned to academia and became dean of the University of Michigan Ross School of Business, a position he held for ten years. In 2002, he served as interim president of the University of Michigan.

White serves on the boards of the American Council on Education, the National Merit Scholarship board, the Evaluation Committee for Chicago's bid to host the Olympic Games, and the Board of Governors of the Argonne National Laboratory. White received an honorary degree from Wabash College in 2003 and the Dr. Martin Luther King Excellence in Leadership Award from the Illinois Commission on Diversity and Human Relations in 2007. He has written, taught, and spoken extensively on leadership and management and is the author of *The Nature of Leadership: Reptiles, Mammals, and the Challenge of Becoming a Great Leader*.

David B. Wiegers

David B. Wiegers was raised in Central Illinois and now lives in Gurnee, Illinois. He has had a life-long interest in Abraham Lincoln. One of his sons shares a birthday with the sixteenth president. Wiegers is an accomplished amateur photographer and has been photographing statues of Abraham Lincoln since 2004. He has visited and photographed over 200 statues commemorating Lincoln and he hopes to publish his work. His Lincoln statue project has been featured in *American Art Review*, the *Chicago Tribune,* and the *Decatur Herald and Review*. Several of his photographs are part of a traveling exhibit entitled *Portraying Lincoln: Man of Many Faces*. Some of his works were used as illustrations in Jim Percoco's book *My Summers with Lincoln.*

George F. Will

George Frederick Will, a Pulitzer Prize-winning conservative American newspaper columnist, journalist, and author, was born on May 4, 1941, in Champaign, Illinois. Will graduated from University Laboratory High School of Urbana, Illinois, and received his B.A. from Trinity College, in Hartford, Connecticut. He received his M.A. from the University of Oxford and his Ph.D. in politics from Princeton University. Will then taught political philosophy at James Madison College, at Michigan State University, and at the University of Toronto. He taught at Harvard University in 1995 and again in 1998. From 1970 to 1972, he served on the staff of Senator Gordon Allott (R-CO). Will served as an editor for the conservative magazine *National Review* from 1972 to 1978. He joined the Washington Post Writers Group in 1979, writing a syndicated twice-weekly column, which became widely circulated among newspapers across the country.

In 1976, Will became a contributing editor for *Newsweek*, writing a biweekly back page column. Among many awards, he has won a Pulitzer Prize for Commentary in 1977. Will has also written two best-selling books on the game of baseball, three books on political philosophy, and has published eleven compilations of his columns for the *Washington Post* and *Newsweek* and of various book reviews and lectures. Will has been a news analyst for ABC since the early 1980s and was a founding member on the panel of ABC's *This Week with David Brinkley* in 1981, now titled *This Week with George Stephanopolous*.

Robert S. Willard

Robert S. Willard is a retired government and industry executive with experience in both market management and information policy advocacy and with a comprehensive knowledge of the application of information technology to public needs. He has served in the federal government as Executive Director of the National Commission on Libraries and Information Science, an independent federal agency whose part-time members advised the President and Congress on the information needs of the American public, and as a senior executive at the Government Printing Office. He has also been responsible for marketing and government relations programs in a number of legal publishing companies. From 1978 to 1985, Willard was Vice President, Government Relations of the Information Industry Association. Earlier, he was a Congressional staffer and an educational fundraiser. Willard was an engineer officer in the U.S. Army with duty in Korea, Vietnam, and the Pentagon from 1966 to 1970.

Willard received the M.S.A. degree in Operations Research and Systems Analysis from George Washington University and the B.S.F.S. degree in International Relations from the Georgetown University School of Foreign Service.

Willard is a long-time collector of books and other material about Abraham Lincoln and has spoken to groups about Lincoln collecting. He is a vice president of The Abraham Lincoln Association, a director (and former president) of The Abraham Lincoln Institute, and Treasurer of the Lincoln Group of the District of Columbia. He was an advisor to the Lincoln Legal Papers project and the Lincoln Digitalization project at Northern Illinois University. In 2005, Willard traveled the Lincoln trail from the birthplace in Hodgenville, Kentucky, through southwestern Indiana to Lincoln's tomb in Springfield, Illinois; in four weeks he covered 1,000 miles, including 200 miles on foot.

Frank J. Williams

Frank J. Williams retired as the Chief Justice of the Rhode Island Supreme Court in 2008. He is the founding chair of the Lincoln Forum and a member of the United States Abraham Lincoln Bicentennial Commission. He has been a leader in the Lincoln community for thirty years, as president of both the Lincoln Group of Boston and The Abraham Lincoln Association. In addition, he is a major collector of Lincolniana, a peripatetic lecturer before Lincoln and Civil War groups, and a scholar whose books include *Abraham Lincoln: Sources and Styles of Leadership* (1994) and *Abraham Lincoln Contemporary* (1995). His latest book, *Judging Lincoln*, is a collection of his lectures and essays. He is also Literary Editor of the *Lincoln Herald* where he contributes a quarterly survey of Lincolniana. Williams served as an Army Captain in Vietnam. On December 30, 2003, he was invited to be a member of the Review Panel for the Military Commissions to be held in Guantanamo Bay, Cuba with the rank of Major General. He resides in Hope Valley, Rhode Island.

Douglas L. Wilson

Douglas L. Wilson taught English and American Literature for thirty-three years at Knox College, where he is now co-director of the Lincoln Studies Center. His work on Abraham Lincoln has appeared in numerous magazines and scholarly journals, including *The Atlantic Monthly, American Heritage*, *Time*, and *The American Scholar*. He has written or edited six books on Lincoln, including three on which he collaborated with Rodney O. Davis: *Herndon's Informants: Letters and Interviews about Abraham Lincoln* (1998); *Herndon's Lincoln* (2006); and *The Lincoln-Douglas Debates (forthcoming).* Two of his books, *Honor's Voice: The Transformation of Abraham Lincoln* (1998) and *Lincoln's Sword: The Presidency and the Power of Words* (2006) won both the Abraham Lincoln Institute Prize and the Lincoln Prize.

Stewart Winger

Stewart Winger took his B.A. in Fundamentals: Issues and Texts from the University of Chicago in 1985. After two years studying political science at the Freie Universitat in Berlin, Germany, he returned to the University of Chicago for his M.A. in 1993 and his Ph.D. in 1998 in History of Culture. His Ph.D. thesis won the prestigious Hay-Nicolay Dissertation Award in 2001 from The Abraham Lincoln Association and the Lincoln Institute of the Mid-Atlantic. After teaching for two years at Purdue University-Calumet, Winger joined the Department of History at the American University in Cairo, Egypt in 1999. His book *Lincoln, Religion, and Romantic Cultural Politics* (2002) won the 2004 Barondess/Lincoln Prize, granted by the Civil War Round Table of New York. He left Egypt in 2003 to become an assistant professor of Humanities and Social Sciences at Lawrence Technological University in Michigan. Winger specializes in American intellectual, cultural, and religious history of the Antebellum Period, offering courses in Civil War and Reconstruction, American Religious History, Religion in the Civil War, and Abraham Lincoln. He is the author of numerous articles and reviews that have appeared in scholarly journals, including *The Journal of the Abraham Lincoln Association*. He joined the history faculty of Illinois State University in 2004.

Kenneth J. Winkle

Kenneth J. Winkle is Sorensen Professor of American History and Chair of the History Department at the University of Nebraska-Lincoln. Born in Cincinnati, Ohio, in 1954, Professor Winkle attended Miami University, where he received a B.A. in History in 1976. He went on to study U.S. History at the University of Wisconsin-Madison, where he studied American political and social history and quantitative historical methods under the direction of Professor Allan G. Bogue. After receiving an M.A. in 1978 and a Ph.D. in 1984, Winkle taught History at Purdue University, Southwest Texas State University, and finally the University of Nebraska. In 1989, his first book, *The Politics of Community: Migration and Politics in Antebellum Ohio*, received the Allan Sharlin Award of the Social Science History Association as the best history book employing social science methods published during the preceding year. He is also author of *The Young Eagle: The Rise of Abraham Lincoln* (2001). He is coauthor with Steven E. Woodworth of *The Oxford Atlas of the Civil War* (2004). Winkle has published his research in *The Journal of Social History*, *The Journal of Interdisciplinary History*, *Civil War History*, *History Teacher*, *The Journal of the Abraham Lincoln Association*, *Social Science History*, *Reviews in American History*, *The Lincoln Newsletter*, and other publications. As a teacher, Winkle has taught more than a dozen different courses in nineteenth-century US history, family history, community history, and quantitative methods.

Laurin A. Wollan, Jr.

Laurin A. Wollan, Jr., of Sweet Briar, Virginia, grew up in Springfield, Illinois, in the company of Lincoln statues. He studied history at Princeton and law at the University of Chicago Law School. At twenty-six, he was an instructor in Millikin University's Department of History and Political Science. Later he was the Assistant Director of the Illinois Sesquicentennial Commission, President of the Sangamon County Historical Society, and speaker (once) at an annual meeting of the American Historical Association. In a quarter-century at Florida State University, his research, writing, and teaching almost always attended to the subject's historical dimension.